Why Lawyers Behave As They Do

New Perspectives on Law, Culture, and Society

ROBERT W. GORDON AND MARGARET JANE RADIN,
SERIES EDITORS

Why Lawyers Behave As They Do, Paul G. Haskell

Thinking Like a Lawyer, Kenneth J. Vandevelde

Intellect and Craft: The Contributions of Justice Hans Linde to American Constitutionalism, edited by Robert F. Nagel

Property and Persuasion: Normativity and Change in the Jurisprudence of Property, Carol M. Rose

Words That Wound: Critical Race Theory, Assaultive Speech, and the First Amendment, Mari J. Matsuda, Charles R. Lawrence III, Richard Delgado, and Kimberlè Williams Crenshaw

Why Lawyers Behave As They Do

PAUL G. HASKELL

UNIVERSITY OF NORTH CAROLINA
LAW SCHOOL

WestviewPress

A Division of HarperCollins*Publishers*

New Perspectives on Law, Culture, and Society

Copyright © 1998 by Westview Press, A Division of HarperCollins Publishers, Inc.

Published in 1998 in the United States of America by Westview Press, 5500 Central Avenue, Boulder, Colorado 80301-2877, and in the United Kingdom by Westview Press, 12 Hid's Copse Road, Cumnor Hill, Oxford OX2 9JJ

A CIP catalog record for this book is available from the Library of Congress.
ISBN 0-8133-6896-0 (hc) — ISBN 0-8133-6897-9 (pb)

The paper used in this publication meets the requirements of the American National Standard for Permanence of Paper for Printed Library Materials Z39.48-1984.

10   9   8   7   6   5   4   3   2   1

To Sally

Contents

Preface   xiii

1   The Behavior of Lawyers   1

    1. Discrediting the Truthful Witness, 2
    2. Exploiting the Adversary's Mistake, 3
    3. Better Not to Probe, 3
    4. Stating the Law Before Asking for the Facts, 4
    5. Dilatory Tactics, 5
    6. Describing the Consequences of Criminal Conduct, 6
    7. Counseling to Breach a Contract, 7
    8. Lying in Negotiations, 8
    9. Custody Blackmail, 9
    10. Using a False Identity, 9
    11. Inserting an Illegal Clause, 10
    12. Taking Advantage of Another Lawyer's Ignorance, 10
    13. Dealing with the Unrepresented Person, 11
    14. Arguing Pro and Con, 12
    15. Confidentiality: Life-Threatening Injury, 12
    16. Confidentiality: Past Fraud, 14
    17. Confidentiality: Child Abuse, 15
    18. Confidentiality: Unprosecuted Homicide, 15
    19. Immoral Objective: Statute of Limitations, 15
    20. Immoral Objective: Television Trash, 16
    21. Immoral Objective: Gambling Enterprises, 16
    22. Immoral Objective: Nazi Speech, 17
    23. Immoral Objective: Seeking Acquittal of a
       Rape-Murderer, 17
    Summary of Principles, 18
    Notes, 22

2   The Lawyer's Service on Behalf of an Immoral Objective   27

    The Elements of Morality, 27
    The Judge and the Immoral Law, 34
    The Role Morality of the Lawyer, 35

Client Autonomy as Moral Justification, 38
The Response to the Lawyer's Role Morality, 40
The Response to the Client Autonomy Justification, 43
Two Special Situations: Breach of Contract and Seeking
    Acquittal for the Rape-Murder, 44
Notes, 46

3   The Morality of the Means   51

Litigation as Fact-Finding, 52
Confidentiality, 56
Tactics, 66
A Contradiction, 75
The Justice Theory of Representation, 75
An Experiment, 76
Notes, 81

4   A Troubled Profession   85

The Hired Gun and the Independent Lawyer, 85
Advertising, 92
Commercialism, 99
Hardball Tactics, 103
Conclusion, 105
Notes, 105

Appendix: Excerpts from Professional Rules   109

RULE 1.2: Scope of Representation (Missouri), 109
RULE 1.3: Diligence (Missouri), 110
RULE 1.5: Fees (Missouri), 110
RULE 1.6: Confidentiality of Information (Missouri), 111
RULE 1.8: Conflict of Interest: Prohibited Transactions
    (Missouri), 111
RULE 1.16: Declining or Terminating Representation
    (Missouri), 111
RULE 2.1: Advisor (Missouri), 112
RULE 3.1: Meritorious Claims and Contentions (Missouri), 112
RULE 3.2: Expediting Litigation (Missouri), 113
RULE 3.3: Candor Toward the Tribunal (Missouri), 113
RULE 3.4: Fairness to Opposing Party and Counsel (Missouri), 113
RULE 3.6: Trial Publicity (Missouri), 113
RULE 4.1: Truthfulness in Statements to Others (Missouri), 114
RULE 4.3: Dealing With Unrepresented Person (Missouri), 114
RULE 4.4: Respect for Rights of Third Persons (Missouri), 115

RULE 7.1: Communications Concerning a Lawyer's Services
(South Carolina), 115
RULE 7.2: Advertising (South Carolina), 115
RULE 7.3: Direct Contact with Prospective Clients
(South Carolina), 116
RULE 8.4: Misconduct (Missouri), 116
RULE 9.1: Definition of Terms (Missouri), 116

Index 117

Preface

We lawyers know that our approval rating is very low these days. Lawyer jokes abound. We tend to attribute this to the excesses of some members of the bar and the media attention they draw, as well as to the caricatures of lawyers in the movies and on television. Unquestionably these circumstances aggravate the condition, but I think the problem is more basic than that. It has to do with how the profession defines itself.

We lawyers are acculturated to accept the model of the lawyer as the loyal servant in pursuit of the client's objective without regard for the interests of or damage inflicted upon others. The professional rules permit the lawyer to wear moral blinders. Many lawyers choose not to practice this way, but the permissibility of this style of practice is not disputed.

I use the word "acculturated" advisedly. For many years, first as a practicing lawyer and then as a law professor, I did not seriously question the appropriateness of this model of behavior, although my visceral reaction to it was negative. The adversary method was an integral part of the Anglo-American system of justice, and despite some of its unfortunate aspects, on balance it was a good thing. My response, I believe, is typical of those who harbor some reservations. The problem is considered to reside in the excesses of some members of the bar.

After many years of teaching and writing devoted primarily to real estate, wills and trusts, ten years ago I decided to try teaching professional ethics. For the first time in my professional life I critically examined the rules that govern lawyers. I combined this with some reading in the field of moral evaluation. I came to the conclusion that a good deal of what lawyers are permitted to do is not morally defensible and is not necessary for the proper functioning of our legal system. Indeed, the system would function better if the rules of the game were changed.

This book is the result. Some lawyers may find my conclusions offensive. I regret this, and I intend no offense. The lawyers who practice in a manner that is criticized in this book do so usually in the belief that it serves the interest of justice. I do not question their good faith. The purpose of this book is to suggest that the professional rules are morally flawed and that there is a better way for lawyers to do their job.

Paul G. Haskell

Why Lawyers Behave As They Do

1

The Behavior of Lawyers

In recent years I have been teaching a course to law students titled "Professional Responsibility," which deals with the rules governing the conduct of lawyers.[1] This subject is also described as legal ethics; the terms are used interchangeably. The term "legal ethics" is misleading, however, because the primary definition of ethics is morality. The secondary definition is the rules of conduct governing a profession. It is the secondary definition that applies here. The professional rules sometimes impose duties that are moral in nature, but many have only attenuated moral significance, if any at all. Indeed, aspects of the lawyer's exclusive dedication to the interests of the client are considered by some moral philosophers to be morally unjustifiable.

In teaching the course I have been struck by the realization that it contains a story that has not been told to the public, at least not adequately. The lawyer in his professional role is perceived by the public as devious and manipulative, perhaps hypocritical or dishonest, and sometimes unconcerned with the harm done to others or to society in general. Lawyers' conduct certainly is not always so, but it is so often enough to justify the perception.

The rules governing lawyers' conduct permit or require such behavior in myriad circumstances. The untold story is the rationale for such conduct. On its face the conduct is immoral or destructive, but it is maintained that there are societal purposes being served, the value of which justifies the behavior. Most in the profession who think about the matter believe this, but not all. The rationale is controversial, as we shall see. If the rationale fails, the behavior is indefensible. The object of this book is to explain the rationale for lawyers' behavior and to assess its validity.

The first step is to describe specifically what the rules governing lawyers require or permit them to do. The examples that follow illustrate how lawyers may or must behave under the professional rules that govern them. The first group of examples describe a variety of tactics, techniques, and practices of lawyers. The next several examples illustrate the consequences of the lawyer's duty to maintain the confidentiality of information acquired in the representation of the client, and the concluding examples deal with the representation of clients who are pursuing objectives that are legal but morally questionable.

1. DISCREDITING THE TRUTHFUL WITNESS

At one o'clock in the morning Mugger knocked a pedestrian to the ground and took his money at a lighted intersection. Witness observed the crime from across the street. Within thirty seconds a patrol car came upon the scene, and Witness described Mugger to the officers. The officers promptly arrested Mugger several blocks away. Mugger protested his innocence when arrested. He was prosecuted for the crime of robbery. Mugger did not testify at the trial; a criminal defendant has the constitutional right not to testify. The prosecutor has the burden at the trial of convincing the jury that the defendant is guilty beyond a reasonable doubt.

Mugger told his lawyer that he committed the act. Witness testified for the prosecution that Mugger was the culprit. In an effort to discredit Witness's testimony, the lawyer on cross-examination brought out that she had several convictions for shoplifting, that she had been drinking for several hours that evening, and that she had had a violent argument with Mugger at a bar earlier in the evening.

The lawyer's conduct is proper; he is permitted to attempt to discredit the testimony of a witness he knows is telling the truth.[2] A lawyer is permitted to advance the objectives of his client by all means within the law and the professional rules. Efforts to discredit the testimony of an opposing witness which is known to be false or the truthfulness of which is in doubt, are, of course, permissible. If a lawyer is not permitted to discredit the testimony of a truthful witness, the client is penalized for telling his lawyer the truth because it is from that information that the lawyer learns that the testimony is truthful.

A lawyer is not permitted to present evidence he knows to be false,[3] but that has not been done here. A lawyer is also not permitted to cross-examine an opposing witness in a manner that has no substantial purpose other than to humiliate or harass,[4] but that has not been done here because the information about Witness that has been disclosed reflects adversely upon her character and the credibility of her testimony. This reasoning may seem sophistic, but it is used to justify a lawyer's efforts to impeach the credibility of an opposing witness under these circumstances. Unquestionably the purpose and effect of such conduct are to blur the truth and mislead the jury.

Here is a similar example. A lawyer represented Killer, who admitted to his lawyer that he committed the homicide for which he was being prosecuted. The prosecution obtained drops of blood from the scene of the crime and submitted them to a laboratory for DNA identification. The laboratory identified the blood as being, in all likelihood, that of Killer. The lawyer cross-examined the laboratory technicians for the purpose of revealing flaws in their procedures, even though she knew the lab's work had produced an accurate result.

The lawyer's conduct is professionally permissible. She is not presenting false evidence; she is merely trying to discredit valid evidence. Again, the consequence may be to blur the truth and mislead the jury.

2. EXPLOITING THE ADVERSARY'S MISTAKE

A lawyer represented Mugger, who was charged with robbery. Mugger told her that he knocked Victim to the ground, stunning him, and stole his watch and wallet. Victim testified that he was robbed at ten o'clock. In fact, the incident occurred at nine o'clock, but Victim's condition and the loss of his watch caused him to lose track of time the night of the crime. Mugger did not testify at his trial, which was his constitutional right. Two of his acquaintances testified truthfully that Mugger was at a bar with them at ten o'clock.

The lawyer is permitted to present that testimony because it is truthful; a lawyer is only forbidden to present evidence that he knows to be false. The fact that the testimony has the effect of obfuscating the truth and misleading the jury makes no difference. A lawyer is entitled to take advantage of the error in the prosecution's case by the use of truthful evidence.[5]

3. BETTER NOT TO PROBE

A lawyer represented Wife in divorce and child custody litigation. The lawyer lived in the same neighborhood as the family and knew the husband slightly. Wife told the lawyer of shocking neglect and psychological abuse of the children, aged 3 and 4, by the husband and stated her intention to testify to this effect. Wife also identified two friends who were prepared to testify that they had observed such abuse and neglect. The lawyer spoke to the friends; they confirmed Wife's statement. The lawyer was skeptical of the truthfulness of these allegations, but he did not probe further to confirm their accuracy; he went ahead and presented the testimony.

The professional rules provide that "A lawyer shall not knowingly . . . offer evidence that the lawyer knows to be false."[6] The definitional section of the rules states that "'Knowingly' . . . denotes actual knowledge of the fact in question."[7] The lawyer did not have actual knowledge that the allegations were false. The lawyer might have discovered that they were false or exaggerated if he had inquired of others, but the rules did not require the lawyer to do this. In this circumstance many lawyers would probe further, but it is common practice not to do so.[8]

4. Stating the Law Before Asking for the Facts

Mother, a widow, died and left a will that disposed of her entire estate to her Daughter. Son, Mother's only other child, was very unhappy. If the will was invalid, under the law Daughter and Son would share the estate equally. Son retained a lawyer for the purpose of contesting the validity of the will. The lawyer told Son that the usual grounds for contesting a will are lack of mental capacity to make a will and undue influence exercised upon the person making the will.

In his business Son had been involved in litigation and knew that if he said something to his lawyer that was damaging to his case, any subsequent modification would be problematic because of the rule that a lawyer is prohibited from presenting evidence that he knows to be false. Before Son provided the lawyer with any facts, Son asked her for a legal definition of mental capacity and undue influence. (The definitions contain a number of elements and are somewhat technical.) The lawyer complied with Son's request, thereby providing Son with information that would enable him to tailor his "recollection" of the facts to suit his best interests, if he were so inclined. That is to say, Son might opt to "recall" events that satisfied the definition of incapacity or undue influence.

Lawyers are permitted to assist witnesses in presenting their testimony in an orderly and convincing manner. Counseling a witness to lie is, of course, impermissible,[9] as is allowing a witness to testify in a manner that the lawyer knows is perjurious. The problematic area is where counseling with respect to the significance or consequences of certain testimony may have the effect of suggesting that the client commit perjury.

The lawyer's conduct here is permissible. Son is entitled to a statement of the law before he tells what he knows. The lawyer is not required to withhold information on the law until after Son has told him the facts. Son may misuse what the lawyer tells him, but that does not make the lawyer's conduct improper. Many lawyers, however, would decline to set out the law before receiving the facts from the client.

Suppose the lawyer initiated the discussion by telling Son that if Mother, who was elderly, was lucid and alert the day she executed the will, incapacity would be difficult to establish, and that if Mother was a strong-willed person, undue influence would be difficult to establish. A statement by the lawyer of the legal consequence flowing from a hypothesized fact, without having been asked about it, may be considered a suggestion that the client create a "fact" to support his case. Such behavior probably violates professional rules.[10]

5 . DILATORY TACTICS

Drug Company produced a popular drug that was used for five years for respiratory ailments. A federal agency had been investigating the effects of the drug on blood pressure; there were strong indications that in the near future distribution of the drug would be prohibited. A number of studies had concluded that the drug had a dangerously adverse effect upon blood pressure in some circumstances, but there were several responsible scientists who were skeptical of the validity of the studies because of the methodologies employed. Drug Company had a large inventory of the drug and would suffer a significant loss if the ban were to be imposed soon.

The lawyer advised the president of Drug Company that he could delay the ban for several months by petitioning for a hearing to present the testimony of the skeptical scientists. The lawyer also told the president that continued sales in this circumstance might increase the potential of liability for harm to consumers of the product. Neither the president nor the lawyer believed that the testimony would prevent the ban from being imposed. The president told the lawyer to petition for a hearing. The lawyer complied with the direction. This action was taken solely to obtain the delay in the application of the ban.

The lawyer's advice and conduct are professionally proper. The rules provide that "A lawyer shall not bring . . . a proceeding . . . unless there is a basis for doing so that is not frivolous."[11] A proceeding is not frivolous "even though the lawyer believes that the client's position ultimately will not prevail."[12] The expert testimony to be offered in the hearing may be the position of only a few scientists, but it is not frivolous.

The rules also prohibit lawyers from engaging in dilatory tactics, but a proceeding that has a substantial purpose other than to delay is permissible despite the fact that it has a dilatory effect.[13] The presentation of the testimony of responsible scientists constitutes a substantial purpose.

The rules provide that "A lawyer . . . may take whatever lawful and ethical measures are required to vindicate a client's cause or endeavor. A lawyer should act with commitment and dedication to the interests of the client and with zeal in advocacy upon the client's behalf."[14] In this context, the term "ethical" means within the rules governing the profession. Conduct that is within the law and within the professional rules is permissible regardless of its consequences. A lawyer may use all legal and professionally permissible means to further the interests of her client.

Although the lawyer's actions are within the rules, many lawyers would decline to comply with the president's decision. It is professionally obligatory to inform the client of the legal options available, but many lawyers would recommend against petitioning for the hearing because of the potential for harm to consumers that may be caused by the delay and because the dilatory purpose impedes the proper functioning of the legal process. If the president nevertheless insisted upon proceeding with the hearing, the lawyer is permitted to decline and terminate the representation of the client.[15]

6. Describing the Consequences of Criminal Conduct

A lawyer represented a manufacturing corporation, whose liquid discharge contained chemicals. The president of the corporation called him in to discuss recent federal regulations dealing with chemical effluents. The lawyer described the operation of the regulations, the willful violation of which could result in criminal prosecution. The president commented that compliance would be very expensive and asked the lawyer what the realities of governmental enforcement were. He responded that in his experience government inspectors who detected a violation usually provided the violator with a period of time within which to come into compliance if the violation did not exceed by more than thirty percent the limits allowed by law. In addition, due to understaffing, the government did not attempt to impose sanctions on violators whose discharge did not exceed the legal maximum by more than fifteen percent.

The lawyer's conduct is professionally permissible. The lawyer is forbidden to "counsel a client to engage, or assist a client, in conduct that the lawyer knows is criminal or fraudulent, but a lawyer may discuss the legal consequences of any proposed course of conduct."[16] The lawyer is permitted to respond to the president's question concerning the realities of enforcement because that is a discussion of the legal consequences of a proposed course of conduct. The lawyer would not be permitted to suggest that the client need not comply with the law, for this would constitute counseling the client to commit a crime.[17] The line between discussing the consequences of criminal or fraudulent conduct and counseling or assisting such conduct is not always clear.

It should also be noted that sometimes the penalty for failure to comply with a governmental regulation is characterized as a civil penalty in the form of a fine rather than as a criminal penalty. The difference between them has to do primarily with the procedural requirements for enforcement. In addition, a crime has greater stigmatizing effect than a civil penalty, both socially and legally. If the only sanction for violation of an environmental regulation is a civil penalty, in most states the lawyer is free to counsel and assist the client with respect to violation.

7. COUNSELING TO BREACH A CONTRACT

Manufacturer and Supplier had a contract that stated that Supplier would furnish raw materials to Manufacturer at a price of two million dollars over five years. They had been operating under the contract for two years. Manufacturer recently discovered another material that was almost as good as the contract material and cost half as much. Manufacturer's president asked his lawyer if there was anything that could be done about its contractual commitment to Supplier. The lawyer asked the president if Supplier had consistently fulfilled its contractual obligations. The president replied that occasionally the deliveries had been late and occasionally the quality had not been up to standard, but most of the time Supplier had been in compliance.

The lawyer advised the president that the instances of Supplier's noncompliance in all likelihood did not entitle Manufacturer legally to terminate the contract. On the other hand, she stated that if Manufacturer terminated, the instances of noncompliance and the expense of litigation could be used as bargaining tools to bring about a settlement with Supplier that, considering the price of alternative materials, would be advantageous to Manufacturer. She also told the president that if Supplier chose not to settle and carried through to litigation, the net financial result, considering legal fees, would be unfavorable. The lawyer told the president that, based on her experience, the odds were great that a satisfactory settlement would be reached. The president decided to inform Supplier that further deliveries would not be accepted. The lawyer agreed to represent Manufacturer in the negotiations.

The lawyer's conduct is permissible under the professional rules. The rules provide that "A lawyer shall not counsel a client to engage, or assist a client, in conduct that the lawyer knows is criminal or fraudulent."[18] The lawyer is counseling her client to breach its contract with Supplier. A breach of contract is not a crime. A crime is an act for which an individual may be prosecuted by the state and, if found guilty, fined or jailed. Breach of contract is only a violation of civil (as distinguished from criminal) law. The party to the contract who commits the breach may be sued by the other party for damages to compensate for the loss occasioned by the breach.

Fraud is a willful misrepresentation that induces reliance. There is no fraud here; there is simply a statement that Manufacturer will no longer perform its side of the contract, which is accurate. Lawyers can counsel or assist clients in breaches of contract as long as neither the client nor the lawyer lies to the other party.

Many lawyers would not participate in the breach of contract. The lawyer has an obligation to tell her client what his options are and what the consequences of those actions may be, but she may recommend that the client perform his legal obligation. If the client chooses to breach, the lawyer can terminate the relationship if she chooses.

8. LYING IN NEGOTIATIONS

(A) A lawyer represented Construction Company, whose employees negligently caused an explosion that damaged an adjacent building. Construction Company clearly was liable; the only issue concerned the amount of damages. Suit was brought against Construction Company. The owner gave the lawyer authority to settle for $600,000. In a negotiating conference with the attorney for the party whose building was damaged, the lawyer made a settlement offer of $400,000. The other party's attorney asked the lawyer if he was authorized to negotiate a settlement for more than that figure. The lawyer responded that he was not.

The lawyer's misrepresentation appears to be professionally permissible. The rules provide that in representing a client a lawyer shall not "knowingly make a false statement of material fact or law to a third person."[19] However, an explanatory comment to the rule states, "Under generally accepted conventions in negotiation, certain types of statements ordinarily are not taken as statements of material fact. Estimates of price or value placed on the subject of a transaction and a party's intentions as to an acceptable settlement of a claim are in this category."[20]

The attorney for the injured party stated that the cost of repairing the building would be about $300,000 and the loss of business would amount to about $200,000. In fact, the attorney was told by his client that the repairs were likely to cost about $200,000, and that the interruption of business would probably cost about $100,000. This statement is probably permissible puffing under the professional rules as an estimate of "price or value placed on the subject of a transaction." The rules seem to accept the ethics of the marketplace in negotiations.

(B) A lawyer represented Owner, whose business was ruined by the wrongful conduct of a bank, causing him substantial economic loss. Owner also suffered some emotional distress, but it was not severe. He got his business back on track and brought suit against the bank. Liability was clear; the only issue was the amount of damages. In negotiations for settlement of the litigation, Owner's lawyer stated that her client suffered severe emotional distress.

This was an exaggeration, but should it be considered a professional violation? In a study conducted several years ago, this question was put to a group of fifteen lawyers (nine law professors, four trial lawyers, and two federal judges). Eight said it was impermissible to make the statement; five said it was permissible; two were equivocal.[21]

9. CUSTODY BLACKMAIL

A lawyer represented Husband in a divorce proceeding. Wife wanted the custody of the children, as well as alimony and child support. Husband had no interest in the custody of the children, and wanted to minimize the alimony and child support. His lawyer advised Husband that a custody demand could be a bargaining device in negotiations to reduce alimony and child support because of Wife's fear of losing exclusive custody of the children. The lawyer told Husband that if Wife called their bluff by not yielding on alimony and child support and insisting on custody, they would withdraw the custody demand. Husband agreed to the strategy, and it turned out as planned—Wife settled for lower alimony and child support in exchange for exclusive custody.

This has been referred to as "custody blackmail." It is often done, and it may be professionally permissible.[22] It is a misrepresentation of Husband's state of mind, but it has become a negotiating convention that may legitimize the tactic under the professional rules.

10. USING A FALSE IDENTITY

A lawyer represented Driver, who was being sued for negligently driving his car, which ran into the plaintiff's car and caused her bodily injury. The plaintiff owned her own business, which required some travel. An aspect of the plaintiff's damage claim was that the injury prevented her from conducting some of her business functions. The lawyer was suspicious of the truthfulness of that aspect of the damage claim and hired a private investigator to check it out.

The lawyer was aware that the private investigator used false identities in the course of making investigations; in many cases it was the only way to obtain the information being sought. In fact, the private investigator used a false identity in this case, which enabled him to obtain information establishing that the business aspect of the plaintiff's damage claim was false, as the lawyer had suspected.

The professional rules prohibit the lawyer from engaging in dishonest or fraudulent conduct.[23] The lawyer's knowledge of the investigator's subterfuge certainly involves him in dishonest conduct. Nevertheless it has been maintained that the broad language of the rules was not meant to cover the use of subterfuge for the purpose of establishing an adversary's falsification.[24] In any event, it is a common practice. Indeed, criminal prosecutors are aware that the police often use undercover agents who misrepresent their identities to detect crime. Acquiescing in the use of a false identity by another to discover the truth may be professionally permissible.

It should be noted that this form of deception serves a different end from the forms of deception described in the other examples. Here the deception is for the purpose of achieving what the client is entitled to under the law; deception more often serves the end of obtaining an advantage to which the client is not entitled under the law.

11. INSERTING AN ILLEGAL CLAUSE

Landlord owned a number of apartment houses. His lawyer prepared a lease form that every tenant must sign. The lease contains a provision to the effect that Landlord has no obligation to make any repairs during the period of the lease or any renewal of the lease. This provision is in conflict with a state statute that requires landlords to make specific repairs and in general to maintain the apartments in a habitable condition—obligations that cannot be modified by the terms of a lease. Landlord and his lawyer are aware of the statute. The tenants never consult a lawyer before signing the lease. Most tenants are unaware of their statutory rights. The purpose of the inclusion of the clause is to discourage tenants from asking for or insisting upon repairs to be made by Landlord.

The professional rules forbid lawyers from assisting their clients in criminal or fraudulent activity and from engaging in dishonest, deceitful, or fraudulent conduct. The inclusion of the provision in the lease is not a crime. This practice is certainly a form of deception, however, as its purpose is to mislead the tenant into believing that the lease denies him any legal claim for repairs. Of course, tenants could discover the invalidity of the provision by consulting a lawyer.

Lawyers often overreach by including in contracts unenforceable provisions favorable to their clients in order to induce or discourage certain conduct when their bargaining position permits it. It is not clear that this relatively mild form of deception is covered by the prohibition against fraudulent, dishonest, and deceitful conduct. Its frequent use and the absence of any specific prohibition in the rules suggest that it is professionally permissible.[25]

12. TAKING ADVANTAGE OF ANOTHER LAWYER'S IGNORANCE

Mechanic replaced the worn brakes on Customer's car. Customer picked up the car and drove off at a speed of 50 miles per hour in a 30-mile-per-hour zone. As he approached a red light at that speed, the brakes malfunctioned and the car swerved, smashing into a tree. Customer was injured and the car was totaled. It was clear that both Customer and Mechanic had been negligent.

The traditional rule had been that a negligent party (defendant) was absolved from liability if the party suing (plaintiff) was also guilty of negligence that contributed to the injury. This was true even if the negligence of the defendant contributed more substantially to the accident than the negligence of the plaintiff. However, in recent years, most states have changed the traditional rule to provide that in circumstances like these the defendant is liable to the plaintiff in accordance with his proportionate share of the responsibility for the accident. That is, if the plaintiff's damages are $100,000, the plaintiff's negligence contributed 20 percent, and the defendant's negligence contributed 80 percent, the defendant is liable for $80,000.

In this case, the state changed the traditional rule six months ago. In the negotiations for settlement of Customer's claim against Mechanic, it became clear to Mechanic's lawyer that Customer's attorney was inexperienced in personal injury work and was unaware of the change in the law. Mechanic's negligence probably contributed 80 percent to the accident, but apparently Customer's attorney believed that any proof of his client's negligence would bar his claim. Mechanic's lawyer did not inform his counterpart of the change in the law. The parties entered into a settlement in an amount that was far less than what Customer would have received had his attorney been aware of the change in the law.[26]

Mechanic's lawyer's silence is professionally permissible. He has no duty to educate the opposing attorney. It should be noted, however, that the professional obligation to a judge is different. The rules provide, "A lawyer shall not knowingly . . . fail to disclose to the tribunal legal authority known to the lawyer to be directly adverse to the position of the client and not disclosed by opposing counsel."[27]

13. Dealing with the Unrepresented Person

A lawyer represented Computer Programming, a company in the business of selling programming services to commercial enterprises. The lawyer prepared a form contract that was very favorable to Computer Programming, dealing with matters of copyright, warranties, and a variety of risks. In most cases the purchaser of the services retains an attorney who negotiates changes in the terms of the contract to make it more balanced. The lawyer intended the form contract to be a starting point for negotiation between lawyers. Occasionally a small businessperson did not retain an attorney and accepted the form contract without any change. The lawyer assumed that such a businessperson did not appreciate the one-sided nature of the contract and the risks to which he was exposed. The lawyer never advised such a businessperson that he should consult an attorney.

The lawyer's conduct is professionally permissible. The rules provide that a lawyer who is dealing on behalf of a client with a person not represented by counsel must not state or imply that the lawyer is looking out for the interests of that person. The rules also state that in this circumstance the lawyer "should not give advice to an unrepresented person other than the advice to obtain counsel."[28] It is permissible to advise the person to obtain counsel but it is not required. Some lawyers would advise a person to consult a lawyer in this circumstance.

14. ARGUING PRO AND CON

A lawyer represented a manufacturer of an appliance in a suit in a state court brought by an injured consumer against the company. In the course of the trial, the lawyer argued for a certain interpretation of an applicable statute. The trial judge accepted that interpretation. On that basis the lawyer obtained a judgment for her client in the trial, and the consumer did not appeal the judgment to a higher court.

Six months later the same lawyer represented another injured consumer in a suit against a different manufacturer of a similar appliance. The case was heard in the same state court but before a different trial judge. This time the lawyer argued for an interpretation of the same statute opposite to the interpretation she had advocated in the prior suit.

The lawyer's reversal of position is permissible. There is no hypocrisy here. Lawyers are not to be identified with the positions they take, nor are they expected to believe in the arguments they make. Lawyers are actors playing roles in the theater of law. A lawyer is obligated to take whatever position the needs of her client require, regardless of inconsistency with positions taken in past litigation. As a matter of business prudence, however, many lawyers would not accept the second representation because of concern for the appearance of disloyalty to the interests of the first client, but this is an entirely different consideration from professional permissibility.

There is a limitation that is applicable here: A lawyer may not take conflicting positions on a legal issue in courts in the same state at the same time. The reasoning here is that the immediacy of the simultaneous conflicting arguments may reduce the chance of success for one client or the other. This would constitute a form of impermissible disloyalty to the client.[29]

15. CONFIDENTIALITY:
LIFE-THREATENING INJURY

Driver negligently drove through a red light and struck Pedestrian. Pedestrian suffered a fractured arm and ribs. Driver was clearly at fault legally; the only issue related to the amount of damages. A physician retained by

Driver's lawyer examined Pedestrian and discovered that in addition to the fractures, Pedestrian suffered an aortic aneurysm that was life-threatening. In light of Pedestrian's medical history and records, there was no doubt the aneurysm was caused by the accident.

The negotiations between Pedestrian's attorney and Driver's lawyer involving the amount of the settlement indicated that Pedestrian, his attorney, and his physician were unaware of the aortic aneurysm. The amount demanded by Pedestrian's attorney did not reflect the life-threatening nature of the injury. The physician hired by Driver's lawyer did not disclose the aneurysm to Pedestrian or his attorney because he considered that the contractual context of his examination preempted any medical ethical obligation that would otherwise apply, committing him to disclose what he knew only to Driver's lawyer. The lawyer for Driver did not disclose the aneurysm because of his duty of loyalty to his client's interests[30] and his duty of confidentiality. Driver's lawyer is obligated to maintain the confidentiality of information acquired in the professional relationship.[31]

Driver's lawyer also represented Driver's insurance company. He asked the senior officer of the insurance company responsible for matters of this nature whether she wanted the aneurysm to be disclosed to Pedestrian. The officer told the lawyer to enter into the settlement at the amount asked by Pedestrian's attorney as soon as possible, and then to disclose the aneurysm to Pedestrian. The lawyer acted in accordance with those instructions.

As a matter of contract law, a party to a settlement agreement is usually not required to disclose information bearing on the settlement that is unknown to the other side, although he may, of course, if he wishes to.[32] The lawyer is bound not to disclose this confidential information under the professional rules unless the client authorizes such disclosure.

The silence of Driver's lawyer endangered Pedestrian's life and resulted in a settlement that inadequately compensated Pedestrian. As we can see, a very high moral price may be paid for the duty of confidentiality. Unquestionably many lawyers would disclose the information immediately upon learning of it; the risk to life would outweigh the professional obligation of confidentiality in the moral scales.

In some states, as a matter of contract law, a party to a settlement agreement may be obligated to disclose information of this nature bearing upon the settlement; if the disclosure is not made, the settlement agreement may be invalidated for failure to disclose. A lawyer must advise the client of this consequence. If the client chooses to remain silent, the lawyer must remain silent pursuant to his duty of confidentiality. It is provided in the professional rules that fraud does not include "failure to apprise another of relevant information."[33] For professional purposes the lawyer's silence in the aneurysm situation does not constitute fraud by him, nor does it constitute assistance of the client in fraudulent conduct.[34]

16. Confidentiality: Past Fraud

Computer, Inc., bought computers and leased them out. Computer financed its purchases with bank loans. A lawyer represented Computer in its dealings with banks for several years. During this time, through the creation of false documents, Computer borrowed from banks for "purchases" of computers that never occurred. The lawyer had no knowledge of the fraud. She and the banks had relied upon certifications by Computer's accounting firm, which had also been deceived.

One day a senior officer of the accounting firm advised the lawyer that Computer had defrauded the banks and that in due course this would be disclosed. When she confronted the president of Computer with this charge, he admitted that wrongs had been committed but assured her that the banks would be paid and that the practice had stopped. Shortly thereafter she terminated her representation of Computer. Computer proceeded to retain another law firm to represent it in future borrowings. The lawyer never told the successor law firm or the banks her reason for terminating her representation. More fraudulent loans were made. The successor law firm had no knowledge of the fraud. Several months later all the fraudulent activity came to light.

The lawyer's failure to advise the successor law firm or the banks of what she knew was proper under the professional rules. She learned of the fraud in connection with her representation of Computer, and she was forbidden to disclose such information without the consent of the client.[35] Confidentiality of information acquired in the professional relationship is a cardinal principle of the profession.

The lawyer's silence in this situation allowed the fraud upon the banks to continue. It also involved the successor law firm in a situation that was potentially damaging; even innocent association with fraudulent activity may affect one's reputation. There was also the possibility that the successor law firm would be charged, however improperly, with complicity in the fraud. Nevertheless, the professional rules place enormous value upon confidentiality of client information. The price for this principle can obviously be very high.

There is an exception to the duty of confidentiality that provides that the lawyer may (not must) reveal the intention of the client to commit a crime and provide the information necessary to prevent it.[36] Acquiring loans by fraud is a crime. The lawyer, in her discretion, would have been permitted to warn others if she believed that the fraudulent practices would continue, but she would not be required to do so.

It should be emphasized that the lawyer's unwitting participation in her client's fraudulent conduct did not violate the professional rules because she did not know that the conduct was fraudulent at the time.[37]

17. CONFIDENTIALITY: CHILD ABUSE

Mother was divorced and had custody of her two children, aged four and six. Her lawyer was assisting her in connection with various financial matters, including securing social service benefits available to her and child support payments from the defaulting father. In the course of the representation the lawyer learned that Mother was unstable and sometimes beat the children. There was a state law that required an individual who learned of child abuse to report the information to a public authority. The law made no reference to the lawyer's duty of confidentiality.

There is a legal issue as to whether such a statute supersedes the lawyer's duty of confidentiality. In a substantial majority of states the professional rules governing lawyers provide that in the absence of a judicial decision to the contrary, it should be presumed that such a law does not supersede the duty of confidentiality.[38]

18. CONFIDENTIALITY: UNPROSECUTED HOMICIDE

A lawyer represented Client, who had been indicted for a homicide. In the course of discussing Client's personal history, the lawyer learned from Client that five years ago he had committed a murder for which another person was convicted and was serving a life sentence. Client was never prosecuted for that crime. The lawyer did not reveal what he had learned to the public authorities. Despite the miscarriage of justice for the imprisoned individual, the lawyer's conduct in this matter was professionally required by her duty of confidentiality to Client.[39]

19. IMMORAL OBJECTIVE: STATUTE OF LIMITATIONS

Investor entered into a contract with Contractor for the construction of an office building. Shortly before construction was to begin, Contractor decided to undertake another project and notified Investor that he wasn't going to perform the contract. Investor made other arrangements for the construction but incurred substantial additional expenses and lost considerable income on account of Contractor's breach of contract. Investor threatened that if Contractor did not compensate him for such losses he would sue. From time to time they discussed a settlement but never agreed on a figure. Negotiations broke down, time passed, and finally Investor contacted an attorney to bring suit.

In all states, there are statutes—known as statutes of limitations—that place a time limit for bringing a law suit. In this state, suit for breach of contract must be brought within two years of the breach. It is up to the person being sued to plead the statute or not, as he sees fit. Investor contacted the attorney two years and five days following the breach. The attorney promptly brought suit, hoping to convince the trial judge that the statutory period should be extended in this instance.

Contractor retained a lawyer who informed Contractor of the two-year statute. Contractor admitted to his lawyer that he had no legal justification for failure to perform the contract. The lawyer asked Contractor if he wanted to litigate the question of damages, settle out of court, or plead the two-year statute of limitations. Pleading the statute is optional for the Contractor. Contractor instructed the lawyer to plead the two-year statute. She complied with the instruction. The trial judge ruled in favor of Contractor.

The best reason for statutes of limitations is to protect the person being sued who is not, or may not, be liable, but has difficulty establishing his defense because of the passage of time; his witnesses may have forgotten, moved, or died, or other evidence may be unavailable or difficult to obtain years after the event. The statutes are unconditional, however, and are available to parties who have no defense and are clearly liable. The unconditional nature of the statutes eliminates the trouble and expense of examining the justification in each case. Its use is often harsh and unfair, as in this case, but that use is allowed under the law. Some lawyers would decline to plead the statute and would opt to withdraw from representation in this circumstance.

20. IMMORAL OBJECTIVE: TELEVISION TRASH

A lawyer was asked by Television Producer to represent him in contract negotiations with a cable television network, directors, actors, writers, and others, in connection with the production of a television series that would emphasize violence, sadism, and promiscuous sex. The lawyer believed that such television fare contributed to anti-social behavior, degraded women, and was culturally decadent. Nevertheless she agreed to represent Television Producer.

The lawyer believed that whatever the nature of the subject of her representation, it was legal, the client was entitled to what the law permitted, and legal representation was necessary to the realization of what the law permitted. Certainly many lawyers would not accept Producer as a client.

21. IMMORAL OBJECTIVE: GAMBLING ENTERPRISES

Recently a state legalized gambling casinos in certain locations. A lawyer represented Casinos, Inc., in all aspects of its legal gambling operations.

The lawyer believed that commercial gambling was exploitative of human weakness, destructive of the character of those who participate, and that the economic benefits to the community did not justify the harm done. Nevertheless he squared representation with his conscience on the grounds that the law permits what Casinos, Inc., was doing, and that if he did not represent Casinos, Inc., some other lawyer would. Representing a cigarette manufacturer would present a similar dilemma, substituting harm to health for harm to character.

22. IMMORAL OBJECTIVE: NAZI SPEECH

A Nazi organization applied for a permit to conduct a march through the downtown area of a suburb that had a substantial Jewish population. Many of those citizens had family members who died in the Nazi holocaust. The marchers planned to carry placards advocating genocide. The city denied the permit. The Nazi organization then retained a lawyer to file suit to require the city to grant the permit.[40]

Although the lawyer was appalled by Nazi ideology, she believed correctly that the freedom-of-speech provision of the First Amendment entitled the Nazi group to a permit. She also believed that everyone, including the Nazi organization, was entitled to what the law allowed. In addition, she believed that if the Nazi group were denied the right to express themselves, there would be a danger that others wishing to voice unpopular but worthy ideas might meet with such denials as well. In the specific instance, although the lawyer's action would further the Nazi ideology, she took the case in service of a broader social objective.

Lawyers are permitted to select their clients, but the professional rules encourage the representation of unpopular clients. Nonetheless, many lawyers would decline to represent the Nazi organization because they would not want to assist in the dissemination of a viewpoint they find to be abhorrent.

23. IMMORAL OBJECTIVE:
SEEKING ACQUITTAL OF A RAPE-MURDERER

Laypersons often ask how a lawyer with any decency can seek to obtain an acquittal for a client who admits to him that he has committed a heinous crime, such as a rape-murderer. As we have stated, the lawyer is not permitted to present evidence that he knows to be false, but he can present evidence whose genuineness he doubts so long as he doesn't *know* it to be false. The lawyer can attempt to cast doubt upon the credibility of a prosecution witness who he knows to be telling the truth, or he may attempt to discredit physical evidence that he knows to be valid, so long as he does not engage in falsification. Are such tactics justifiable? Most lawyers think they are. Most lawyers also believe that representation of the guilty is justifiable.

Conviction for committing a serious crime is devastating. For that reason, in a criminal case, the prosecution is required to prove beyond a reasonable doubt that the defendant has committed the crime, the jury must be unanimous in concluding that the defendant is guilty, and the defendant cannot be forced to testify. Our social philosophy accepts that it is better to have a guilty person go free under this standard than to have an innocent person be convicted under a lesser standard. (By contrast, in a civil—that is, noncriminal—suit, the jury need only find that the plaintiff has proved his case by a preponderance of the evidence, i.e., that it is more likely than not that the plaintiff's account is true.)

The defendant is entitled to whatever the law allows. The law requires that the state prove guilt beyond a reasonable doubt. The lawyer for the defendant sees to it that the defendant gets what the law allows, and the law allows him to go free if the state is unable to prove guilt in accordance with the standard. The system is designed to protect the innocent defendant, but the guilty defendant often gets the benefit of it also. Once again, better that the guilty go free than an innocent be convicted.

Many lawyers do not find criminal defense work attractive for a variety of reasons; the defense of the guilty is definitely one of them. Such lawyers believe that it is fine for some other lawyer to defend the guilty, because they accept the social principle underlying such representation, but they do not want to be a part of it.

SUMMARY OF PRINCIPLES

The behavior described in the preceding examples is founded upon three interrelated principles: (1) The lawyer's relationship to the client is that of an agent and fiduciary exclusively and zealously dedicated to the advancement of the client's interests; (2) the lawyer is unconcerned with the morality or social consequences of the client's objective; and (3) the lawyer may use all means within the professional rules to achieve the client's objective, regardless of their impact upon others or their relationship to justice.

Almost two centuries ago, in his defense of Queen Caroline, Lord Brougham portrayed the lawyer as an advocate who

> . . . in the discharge of his duty knows but one person in all the world, and that person is his client. To save that client by all means and expedients, and at all hazards and costs to other persons, and, amongst them, to himself, is his first and only duty; and in performing this duty he must not regard the alarm, the torments, the destruction which he may bring upon others.[41]

The professional rules express this position more moderately:

A lawyer should pursue a matter on behalf of a client despite opposition, obstruction or personal inconvenience to the lawyer, and may take whatever lawful and ethical measures are required to vindicate a client's cause or endeavor. A lawyer should act with commitment and dedication to the interests of the client and with zeal in advocacy upon the client's behalf.[42]

The examples discussed are illustrative of the lawyer's exclusive and zealous dedication to the client's interests. The lawyer may assert a claim or position for which there is some factual or legal basis however remote the possibility that the claim or position will be sustained by a court or other arbiter and without regard to the cost that may be inflicted upon others by such an assertion or any dilatory effects the assertion may have.

The lawyer may counsel and assist the client in the violation of law as long as the client is not engaged in conduct that constitutes a crime or that constitutes fraud (misrepresentation or other form of deception). Consequently, the lawyer may counsel or assist the client in committing a breach of contract, engaging in negligent behavior, or violating regulations or statutes that carry only civil penalties because such conduct is neither criminal nor fraudulent.

Although the lawyer is forbidden to counsel or assist the client in conduct that is criminal or fraudulent, the lawyer may inform the client of the potential consequences of conduct contemplated by the client that is criminal or fraudulent, including whether there is significant likelihood of detection and what the severity of possible criminal sanctions (fines or incarceration) might be. Clearly the statement of the potential consequences of criminal or fraudulent activity may in certain circumstances induce such activity.

The lawyer may not present evidence that he *knows* is false, but he may present evidence that he suspects, but does not know, is false. The lawyer may prepare his client or a witness for his client by telling him what the law is on the matter in question before asking him about what happened. This allows the lawyer to convey to the client or witness the consequences of his recollection of events. The lawyer may advise the client or witness to respond to questions from opposing counsel as narrowly as possible and to avoid volunteering information; an excess of truth may be damaging. The lawyer may attempt to impeach the credibility of opposing witnesses that he knows are telling the truth. The lawyer may make an argument to a judge or jury based on evidence that the lawyer does not believe is true, but does not *know* to be false.

Although the lawyer is generally forbidden to lie, in negotiations she is permitted to misrepresent the value of the subject matter of a transaction and to misrepresent the authorization she has received from her client with respect to settlement as well as her client's intentions with respect to settlement.

The lawyer may decline to alert an unrepresented person to the need for legal assistance to avoid risks to which that person may unwittingly be subjecting himself. In dealing with an attorney for an opposing party, the lawyer may decline to alert his counterpart to recent changes in the law of which his counterpart is obviously uninformed, even though that knowledge is essential to the proper representation of his counterpart's client. The lawyer is generally free to exploit the ignorance or mistakes of opposing counsel.

Subject to several exceptions, the lawyer must not disclose information obtained in the representation of her client, without regard to the physical or financial harm that may result to an opposing party or to third parties because that information has been withheld. One exception is that the lawyer may (but need not) disclose the client's intention to commit a crime in the future. Another exception is that the lawyer may disclose information necessary to collect her fee or to enable the lawyer to defend herself against charges stemming from the representation of her client. Another is that the lawyer must disclose that her client intends to testify perjuriously and that evidence she has previously presented believing it at that time not to be false, is, in fact, false.

The lawyer may seek to achieve the lawful objective of his client regardless of the immoral or socially harmful nature of that objective.

It is emphasized that most of the conduct described above is permitted but not required. Many lawyers would not assert marginal claims or participate in a breach of contract. Many lawyers probe their clients to determine the facts, rather than accepting the client's self-serving statements at face value. Many lawyers would advise an unrepresented adversary to hire a lawyer. Many lawyers would not attempt to impeach the credibility of an opposing witness the lawyer knows is telling the truth. Many lawyers would not lie in negotiations. Many lawyers would not represent a client whose objective is socially harmful. Nonetheless, the various practices that have been described are widespread in the profession.

There is language of moderation in the professional rules. There are several references to the appropriateness of advice that goes beyond strictly legal advice. For example: "In rendering advice, a lawyer may refer not only to law but to other considerations such as moral, economic, social and political factors that may be relevant to the client's situation."[43]

There is also recognition that the lawyer is not required to go the limit in her exclusive and zealous dedication to the client's interests: "A lawyer should act with commitment and dedication to the interests of the client and with zeal in advocacy upon the client's behalf. However, a lawyer is not bound to press for every advantage that might be realized for a client."[44]

The professional rules make it clear that the client has the final decision concerning the objectives of the representation, such as the terms of the contract that is being negotiated, whether to bring a law suit, or whether to settle a pending suit and what the terms of that settlement should be. The lawyer has the final decision with respect to the means used in pursuit of the objective, but she is obligated to consult with the client.[45] With respect to means, the rules also provide that the lawyer "should defer to the client regarding such questions as the expense to be incurred and concern for third persons who might be adversely affected."[46]

We should also emphasize that there are firm constraints upon the conduct of lawyers. The lawyer is forbidden to lie (except in negotiations); to assist the client in criminal or fraudulent conduct; to present evidence known to be false; to destroy evidence in litigation; to commit crimes involving moral turpitude; to assert frivolous claims; or to use tactics that have no justification in fact or law solely for the purpose of harassment or delay. There are many opportunities legitimately available to the lawyer to mislead or harm others, but there are ultimate limits to the deception and harm that the lawyer is permitted to effect.

The Anglo-American system of freedom under law is the finest form of governance in human history. It imposes order as well as limitations upon state power that assure intellectual, aesthetic, spiritual, and economic freedom. It provides for the orderly transition of power based on majoritarian principles. It includes a system of fundamentally just substantive and procedural principles for the resolution of disputes between individuals and between individuals and the state. In sum, it creates a balance between authority and liberty that honors both community and individual dignity. It has been durable, resilient, and adaptive. It is indeed a system of wise restraints that make men free.

Every orientation program for incoming law students speaks of the contribution of the profession to the development of our remarkable system of governance and of the profession's service on behalf of civil rights, the less fortunate, and the environment. It is all true.

There is, of course, a less glamorous but no less worthy side. Many lawyers serve society in ways that go unheralded, rarely, if ever, compromising personal ethics in the process. They assist in the transfer of property, prepare wills and assist in the planning and administration of estates, and prepare and negotiate contracts in an atmosphere of compromise and accommodation. They assist in the creation of business enterprises and counsel in dealings between parties in a spirit of fairness and candor. If disputes arise they try to settle them in an equitable manner; if settlement efforts fail, they conduct litigation in a manner that minimizes offense and assists in a just resolution.

The practice of law at its best is a caring and productive profession. In the courtroom it can determine truth and achieve justice. In personal matters it can provide security and harmony. In commercial affairs it can facilitate the production of wealth. It can protect the individual and the environment from the misuse of power by the state and private interests.

Then there is what may be viewed as the dark side of the practice of law, in which the lawyer serves the unworthy objective of his client, or employs deception and obfuscation, or harms others in the course of serving the client's objective, whether good, bad, or indifferent. Is such conduct worthy of a profession? Can such conduct be justified in moral or social terms? We now deal with the responses to these questions.

Notes

1. In 1908 the American Bar Association (ABA) promulgated the Canons of Professional Ethics. The ABA is a private organization that has no legal authority over the profession. The Canons constituted a recommendation to the states and many adopted them, usually by action of the highest court of the state, sometimes by the legislature. In 1969 the ABA promulgated the Model Code of Professional Responsibility, replacing the 1908 Canons. Almost all states adopted the Model Code, which was much more detailed than the Canons. In 1983 the ABA promulgated the Model Rules of Professional Conduct, replacing the 1969 Model Code; a number of substantive changes were made, but for the most part the differences were in style and form. The 1983 Model Rules have been adopted in about three-fourths of the states. Throughout this book the 1983 Model Rules are used as the basis for discussion. The Model Rules referred to in the text are contained in the Appendix.

2. This practice by criminal defense counsel is defended by a prominent commentator on legal ethics, Monroe Freedman, in his book Understanding Lawyers' Ethics 161–171 (Matthew Bender, 1990). Another authority, Charles W. Wolfram, in Modern Legal Ethics 651 (West, 1986), suggests that this practice may be justified in criminal defense, but should not be professionally permissible in civil trials. There is no doubt, however, that it is professionally permissible in the civil trial as well. The use of this tactic by criminal defense counsel is supported in the American Bar Association Standards Relating to the Administration of Criminal Justice, The Defense Function § 4–7.6(b). Those same Standards dealing with The Prosecution Function § 3–5.7(b) provide that it is impermissible for the prosecutor to use this tactic. The prosecutor's role "is to seek justice, not merely to convict" § 3–1.2(c). The American Bar Association Standards Relating to the Administration of Criminal Justice are not part of the formal rules of professional behavior such as the 1983 Model Rules, but are intended to provide unofficial guidance to practitioners and courts in the area of criminal justice.

3. Model Rule 3.3(a)(4).

4. Model Rule 4.4.

5. Ethics committees of state bars issue opinions on actual ethical problems presented to them by lawyers. This problem reflects the facts and conclusions of Michigan Ethics Opinion CI–1164 (1987).

6. Model Rule 3.3(a)(4).

7. Model Rules, Terminology.

8. Federal courts and most state courts have a procedural rule in civil cases that the lawyer filing a pleading or a motion must undertake a reasonable inquiry concerning the facts stated in the pleading or motion. (Rule 11 of Federal Rules of Civil Procedure.) Accepting the client's story without further inquiry may not suffice unless it is impracticable to verify through other sources. It is emphasized that this duty is limited to documents filed in a court proceeding. Corroboration by the client's two friends would satisfy this rule. The court may sanction the lawyer monetarily for violation of the rule. The Model Rules of Professional Conduct do not contain any provision requiring investigation of the client's story.

9. Model Rule 3.4(b).

10. Model Rule 1.2(d) and 3.4(b). The practices described in this problem are disapprovingly discussed in Marvin Frankel, Partisan Justice 16 (Hill & Wang, 1980), and Charles W. Wolfram, Modern Legal Ethics 648 (West, 1986). Monroe Freedman takes a more sympathetic view of telling the client the law before asking for the facts in his book Understanding Lawyers' Ethics 155–160 (Matthew Bender, 1990).

11. Model Rule 3.1.

12. Model Rule 3.1, Comment.

13. Model Rule 3.2, Comment.

14. Model Rule 1.3, Comment.

15. Rule 11 of the Federal Rules of Civil Procedure applicable to civil suits in federal courts provides that a pleading or a motion must have some basis in fact and law, and must not have been filed for an improper purpose such as delay. Most state courts have adopted the same rule. The court may impose monetary sanctions against the lawyer for violation. Literally this rule states that a pleading or motion that has a basis in fact and law but which is filed for dilatory purposes would be sanctionable. Except in unusual circumstances, however, this rule has generally been interpreted to mean that a pleading or motion which is not frivolous (i.e., has some substantive basis) is not a violation although delay may be the motivation.

This problem is patterned after one presented in Alan H. Goldman, The Moral Foundations of Professional Ethics 102 (Rowman & Allenheld, 1980).

16. Model Rule 1.2(d).

17. Model Rule 1.2(d).

18. Model Rule 1.2(d).

19. Model Rule 4.1(a).

20. Model Rule 4.1, Comment.

21. Larry Lempert, *In Settlement Talks, Does Telling the Truth Have Its Limits?* 2 Inside Litigation 1 (Prentice-Hall Law and Business, 1988).

22. For a discussion of this technique and its prevalence, see Richard Neely, *The Primary Caretaker Parent Rule: Child Custody and the Dynamic of Greed,* 3 Yale Law and Policy Review 168, 177–79 (1984). See also Jane B. Singer and William L. Reynolds, *A Dissent on Joint Custody,* 47 Maryland Law Review 497, 515–516 (1988); Lenore J. Weitzman, The Divorce Revolution 310 (Free Press, 1985); Eleanor E. Maccoby and Robert H. Mnookin, Dividing the Child 154–59 (Harvard, 1992).

The American Academy of Matrimonial Lawyers has published a set of standards for matrimonial lawyers entitled Bounds of Advocacy (1991). These standards are stated to be "ethical standards . . . that go beyond those required by the American Bar Association and state ethics codes." In essence, they are recommendations to the bar in that area of practice. One of the standards (§ 2.25) states that "An attorney should not contest child custody or visitation for either financial advantage or vindictiveness."

23. Model Rules 8.4, 4.1(a).

24. This is the position taken by Robert E. Keeton, formerly professor of law at Harvard, and currently Federal District Judge, in his book Trial Tactics and Methods 326 (Little, Brown, 2d ed. 1973).

25. The only formal ethics opinion that has been found on this point states that the inclusion of a clause in a legal document that is clearly contrary to law is unethical as a deception to the other party and as a form of disloyalty to the law. Association of the Bar of the City of New York and the New York County Lawyers Association, Committee on Professional Ethics, Opinions on Professional Ethics 435–36 (1956) (Opinion No. 722, December 6, 1948). The 1908 Canons of Professional Ethics were in effect at the time.

26. This problem is patterned after one presented in Alan H. Goldman, The Moral Foundations of Professional Ethics 103 (Rowman & Allenheld, 1980).

27. Model Rule 3.3(a)(3).

28. Model Rule 4.3, Comment.

29. See Model Rule 1.7, Comment.

30. Model Rule 1.3, Comment.

31. Model Rule 1.6.

32. Restatement 2d of Contracts § 161 (1981); Restatement 2d of Torts § 551 (1977); Charles W. Wolfram, Modern Legal Ethics 722 (West, 1986); E. Allan Farnsworth, Contracts § 4.11 (Little, Brown, 1990); William L. Prosser and W. Page Keeton, Law of Torts § 106 (West, 5th ed., 1984).

33. Model Rules, Terminology.

34. This problem is patterned after the case of Spaulding v. Zimmerman, 263 Minn. 346, 116 N.W.2d 704 (Minnesota Supreme Court 1962).

35. Model Rule 1.6(a).

36. Model Rule l.6(b)(1) permits the lawyer to reveal information to prevent the client "from committing a criminal act that the lawyer believes is likely to result in imminent death or substantial bodily harm." Intention to commit a financial or commercial crime cannot be revealed. However, a majority of states permit the lawyer to reveal the client's intention to commit any crime.

37. Model Rule 1.2(d). This problem is derived from the story of O.P.M. Leasing Services, Inc., whose frauds are described in Geoffrey C. Hazard, Susan P. Koniak, and Roger C. Cramton, The Law and Ethics of Lawyering 300 (Foundation Press, 1994).

38. Model Rule 1.6, Comment. See Robert P. Mosteller, Child Abuse Reporting Laws and Attorney-Client Confidences: The Reality and the Specter of Lawyer as Informant, 42 *Duke Law Journal* 203 (1992).

39. A lawyer was faced with this problem following the notorious conviction in Georgia of Leo Frank, a Jewish factory owner, for the murder of his 14-year old employee, Mary Phagan. Frank was sentenced to death. Later Arthur Powell, an Atlanta attorney, was told by a client that he had committed the murder, not Frank. Powell told the Governor of Georgia that he knew Frank was innocent but did not disclose his source. The Governor commuted Frank's sentence to life in prison.

Shortly thereafter a lynch mob hanged Frank. Arthur G. Powell, Privilege of Counsel and Confidential Communication, 6 *Georgia Bar Journal* 334 (1944); Leonard Dinnerstein, The Leo Frank Case 125 (Columbia, 1987); Robert S. Frey and Nancy Thompson-Frey, The Silent and the Damned: The Murder of Mary Phagan and the Lynching of Leo Frank 85–99 (Madison, 1988).

40. This problem is based on the case of Collin v. Smith, 578 F.2d 1197 (7th Circuit Court of Appeals 1978), certiorari denied, 439 U.S. 916 (1978), in which it was held that such speech was protected under the First Amendment.

41. 2 Trial of Queen Caroline 5 (Shackell and Arrowsmith, 1821).

42. Model Rule 1.3, Comment.

43. Model Rule 2.1.

44. Model Rule 1.3, Comment.

45. Model Rule 1.2(a).

46. Model Rule 1.2, Comment.

2

The Lawyer's Service
on Behalf of
an Immoral Objective

The Elements of Morality

The conduct of lawyers described in Chapter 1 frequently harms or deceives others or impedes justice; such behavior is immoral unless it is instrumental in the achievement of some good that outweighs it. In recent years moral philosophers and philosophically inclined law professors have analyzed the question of whether such conduct of lawyers is morally justifiable and have arrived at differing conclusions. We shall examine their reasoning in this chapter.

To understand the moralists, it is necessary first to provide some background concerning the nature of morality and the problem of moral conflicts. The British moral philosopher, Geoffrey F. Warnock, describes the role of morality:

> The general object of moral evaluation must be to contribute . . . to the amelioration of the human predicament. . . . Accordingly, I take it to be necessary . . . to consider, first, what it is in the human predicament that calls for amelioration, and second, what might reasonably be suggested . . . as the specific contribution of "morality" to such amelioration. . . .
>
> . . .
>
> The "general object" of morality . . . is to contribute to betterment—or nondeterioration—of the human predicament, primarily and essentially by seeking to countervail "limited sympathies" and their potentially most damaging effects. It is the proper business of morality, and the general object of moral evaluation . . . to expand our sympathies, or, better, to reduce the liability to damage inherent in their natural tendency to be narrowly restricted.[1]

In sum, human beings tend to be unsympathetic to their fellows, and the function of morality is to correct for that tendency.

Warnock states that our "limited sympathies" for others cause us to harm, deceive, discriminate against, and avoid helping others. He then posits the basic moral principles of nonmaleficence, beneficence, nondeception, and fairness. Nonmaleficence is the avoidance of doing harm; beneficence is the doing of good; nondeception is telling the truth and keeping promises; fairness is nondiscrimination (i.e., differential treatment of individuals requires justification).[2] Other philosophers have referred to the duty of nondeception as the duty of fidelity and to the duty of fairness as the duty of justice; that is how we will refer to these two principles.

There is a consensus among contemporary moral philosophers that nonmaleficence, beneficence, fidelity, and justice are the fundamental components of morality.[3] The philosophical basis for these moral principles is often not explicitly stated, but there are several prominent schools of thought on the question.

Some moralists are utilitarians. The utilitarian defines moral conduct as that which achieves the greatest possible balance of pleasure or happiness over pain, or the greatest net utility, for all concerned, however one defines pleasure, happiness, pain, and utility and however one quantifies such qualities.[4] As we shall see, morality is not a science. The concepts of nonmaleficence, beneficence, fidelity and justice are important themes in utilitarian analysis.

Some moral philosophers are described as intuitionists. They believe that the moral principles are axiomatic, self-evident. How can breaking a promise be other than morally wrong? How can doing harm without good reason be other than morally wrong? How can treating two people differently without a sound reason for it be morally right?[5]

The American philosopher, John Rawls, has expressed the relationship of utilitarianism and intuitionism as follows:

> We sometimes forget that the great utilitarians, Hume and Adam Smith, Bentham and Mill, were social theorists and economists of the first rank; and the moral doctrine they worked out was framed to meet the need of their wider interests and to fit into a comprehensive scheme. Those who criticized them often did so on a much narrower front. They pointed out the obscurities of the principles of utility and noted the apparent incongruities between many of its implications and our moral sentiments. But they failed, I believe, to construct a workable and systematic moral conception to oppose it. The outcome is that we often seem forced to choose between utilitarianism and intuitionism. Most likely we finally settle upon a variant of the utility principle circumscribed and restricted in certain ad hoc ways by intuitionistic constraints.[6]

There are, of course, other theories of the basis for moral principles. The German philosopher, Immanuel Kant, developed the idea that moral principles were logically imperative and absolute, not subject to modification or qualification regardless of circumstances. For example, the duty to tell the truth is binding regardless of the harm that may be avoided or the good that may be achieved by telling a lie in a particular circumstance.[7] As we shall see, the utilitarians and intuitionists allow for violation of the basic moral principles if the circumstances are sufficiently compelling to justify it.

There are those who hold to the social contract theory of morality, the idea that morality consists of a set of rules governing behavior that people implicitly accept for their own protection and benefit.[8] Religious moralists believe that divine revelation is the source of moral truth.[9] There are moralists who reason that moral principles are to be found in the natural law, which contains the conditions that are essential to the development and realization of man's nature.[10] There are also "situationists," who question the validity of any generalized moral principles and determine morality exclusively on the basis of the facts of the specific situation.[11]

Most moral philosophers are concerned primarily with the examination of the theories of morality rather than the analysis of the morality of specific conduct. The analysis of specific conduct is sometimes referred to as "applied ethics" or as "applied morality." Sissela Bok, the author of a significant work in applied morality dealing with lying, has stated:

> The striking fact is that, though no moral choices are more common or more troubling than those which have to do with deception in its many guises, they have received extraordinarily little contemporary analysis. The major works of moral philosophy of this century, so illuminating in other respects, are silent on the subject. . . .
>
> It is difficult to understand all the reasons why so few efforts have been made to analyze our everyday dilemmas of truth-telling. The great distance which so often separates philosophers from applied concerns of any kind provides a partial answer. In philosophy, as elsewhere, professionalization has brought in its wake a vocabulary, a theoretical apparatus, and academic boundaries forbidding to outsiders and confining for those within.[12]

Although in general applied morality has not received adequate attention from academic philosophers, considerable work has been done in recent years in applied morality with respect to biomedical problems.[13] A limited amount of work has also been done concerning the legal profession. The "applied moralists" do not dwell on the theories of morality; indeed, they often do not mention the subject. Their thinking, however, necessarily is founded on some theory of morality, whether stated or unstated.

Our focus here, of course, is on applied morality. It is safe to say that the reasoning of most contemporary applied moralists is a mix of utilitarian and intuitionist considerations, as Rawls stated. Because the quantification theoretically required for utilitarianism is more a figure of speech than a quantitative calculation and because intuitionism posits self-evidence, moral discourse is an art—not a science. The fact that morality does not lend itself to precise measurement does not minimize its significance. Man is a social being, and morality is essential to social organization. Civilization does not exist without the constraint of morality. As a colleague of mine once said in a casual conversation, "Most things that are important in life are indeterminate."

The fundamental moral principles of nonmaleficence, beneficence, justice, and fidelity are the starting points for moral judgment. If a thug knocks you down and steals your wallet, the moral principle of nonmaleficence has been violated and nothing more need be said. If an employer considers only white applicants for positions and rejects all nonwhite applicants regardless of qualifications, the moral principle of justice has been violated and nothing more need be said. If a merchant lies to a customer to induce him to buy his goods, the principle of fidelity has been violated and nothing more need be said.

These are unambiguous examples of immoral conduct, but sometimes behavior that is harmful, discriminatory, or dishonest has a purpose that may make it morally justifiable. For example, I may injure another in the course of defending myself against his assault. In war each nation kills the opponent's citizens. I pay the college tuition of my children, but I do not pay the college tuition of my neighbor's children who are in need and who are just as worthy as my children. A physician lies to a psychologically fragile patient about his medical prognosis because she fears the impact of the truth. Moral judgment may become problematic when there are contextual considerations that may justify the harm, the discrimination, the lie, or the broken promise.

Contemporary moralists do not accept the moral duties as absolutes; there is a presumption that they are to be fulfilled but circumstances may justify their breach. The intellectually challenging moral questions deal with the justifications for harm, lies, broken promises, and discrimination.[14]

For purposes of the moral duty of nonmaleficence, harm is any injury to or interference with the freedom, person, or property of an individual that is not justified in the circumstances. Striking another in self-defense certainly is morally justified. Most accept that the killing by United States armed forces in World War II was morally justified. Most accept that zoning restrictions upon the uses of land and restrictions upon the sale of corporate securities are morally permissible because of their societal objectives. A large majority of Americans accept capital punishment for murder to be morally justifiable.

The duty of fidelity includes more than explicit promises and explicit misrepresentations. The bearing of a child carries a commitment to raise and support that child. Deception includes silence and conduct that has the effect of deceiving others. There may be circumstances, however, in which misrepresentation is morally permissible or even obligatory. If A asks me where B is, and I have good reason to believe that A intends to harm B physically, my untruthful answer to A is morally permissible or obligatory. The president or a military leader is morally permitted or obligated to lie to the press about the location of military personnel in order to protect them. A parent may be justified in lying to a child about the quality of a child's performance in order to sustain the child's confidence.

The duty of justice—that is, giving each what he is entitled to and treating individuals in similar circumstances in a similar manner—is a vast subject. It requires the justification of the differential treatment of individuals, whether that be evidenced through the distribution of goods, jobs, education, or medical services, or by the regulation of conduct. The formal principles are simple enough, but the substance can be complex, varying with societal values.

The classical liberal ideal of equality of opportunity and distribution based on performance, without significant state involvement, is different from the welfare-state emphasis upon distribution based on need. Rawls's position is that inequalities are justified only if they benefit all.[15] Criminal justice, of course, calls for equal treatment under the law; what is also important from the standpoint of justice is the substance of the criminal laws. That is to say, injustice can consist of immoral laws—laws that proscribe certain conduct without adequate justification—as well as disparate administration of the laws.

Beneficence is the duty to do good to others "provided that one can do so without excessive risk or loss to oneself."[16] This qualification follows from the fact that I am as morally valuable as you. I am therefore not obligated to deprive myself in order to provide for you, although I have a duty to provide for you if it does not result in a substantial deprivation to myself. Doing good to others in excess of such an obligation is, of course, considered to be a highly moral act, but it is not a moral duty; such saintly conduct is referred to as supererogatory.

Let us now consider two situations involving moral conflicts, or dilemmas, to illustrate the process of moral analysis. The first concerns deception. Professor is a law professor. Student is in his final year of law school and is in the process of interviewing for a job. He is very personable and interviews well. Student was in two of Professor's courses and received a grade of "B" in both. Student's average places him in the top quarter of his class. He was frequently absent from Professor's classes and was unprepared on the several occasions when Professor called on him in class. Professor also heard from a colleague that Student handed in a seminar paper six weeks late without adequate justification. Professor's impression of Student was that he had not been responsible in the performance of his academic duties, although he was very competent.

Professor received a phone call from Lawyer, a former student whom she had not seen for ten years and whom she knew well when Lawyer was a student. Lawyer said that he was chairperson of his firm's hiring committee, that his firm (a prominent one in a large city) had interviewed Student, and that the firm was very favorably impressed with his academic record and with him as a person. Lawyer asked if Professor knew Student, and if so, what her assessment of him was. Professor knew that if she accurately stated her assessment of Student and her reasons for it, however she might qualify them, Student's chances of receiving an offer would be jeopardized. Professor told Lawyer that Student was in two of her courses in which he had received a good grade, but beyond that she had no other information. Was Professor's response morally justifiable?

The issue, of course, is whether Professor's failure to disclose what she knew, a form of deception, was justified. She failed to disclose in order to help Student, or at least not to harm him. One of the several consequences of lying is that the listener may be harmed by his reliance upon what he has been told. That consequence may apply here. Professor felt, however, that her impression of Student's irresponsibility may have been based upon inadequate experience with Student. Professor also felt that Student might conduct himself responsibly in a job despite his irresponsibility in the law school setting. Professor could have avoided misrepresentation by stating that she preferred not to comment on Student; this, of course, would have damaging implications.

If Professor's impression of irresponsibility is accurate, Lawyer's firm may be harmed by Professor's misrepresentation. If, on the other hand, Student's conduct was due to immaturity or his attitude toward law school and his performance at the firm turns out to be satisfactory, the misrepresentation would harm neither Student nor the firm but would rather benefit both.

The issue is whether the lie is justified by the good that it may produce or the harm that it may avoid. If we begin with a strong presumption that deception is impermissible, it seems that the purported justification is inadequate. However, a conclusion to the contrary would not be unreasonable.

Let us examine a problem dealing with promises. Jim was a bright, young systems analyst employed by Corporation, a large national enterprise. Corporation offered to pay Jim's tuition and living expenses at a leading graduate school of business for the two years required for an M.B.A. In exchange, Jim was to agree to remain in a management position with Corporation for five years after he received his degree. Jim accepted the offer, signed the contract, and started his business school education.

During his first year he met, fell in love with, and married Mary, a young law professor at a nearby law school, an institution of middle-level status. Within weeks of the marriage Mary received an offer to visit (a one-year appointment) during the next academic year at one of the leading law schools in the nation, located 500 miles away. She accepted the offer. During the next academic year they had a commuter marriage, seeing each other most weekends. In the late fall of that year she was offered a tenure-track position at the leading law school, which she accepted. Also during that year she became pregnant, despite their precautions.

Jim had insisted that Mary not accept the tenure-track position, but she did anyway. Mary then insisted that Jim move to her location, find a job there, and help care for the child after it arrived. Jim protested that he was committed to Corporation, which had no offices near her location. Mary responded that her job was a once-in-a-lifetime career opportunity, Corporation would survive without him, and he owed it to the child to move. Mary was adamant about the matter.

Corporation told Jim that he was honor-bound to comply with the contract, but that it would not pursue any legal action if he left. Jim told Corporation that he would repay the firm over time for the cost of his education. Corporation responded that it was the services of bright, young people that it needed. Jim left Corporation, joined Mary, found a job there, and shared the responsibility of caring for the child.

Was Jim's conduct morally acceptable? He broke his promise to Corporation, but was this decision justified by his duties to Mary and the child? Jim's duty to the child is not a case of an altruistic doing of good. Jim came under obligation to the child because he fathered the child. Jim's relationship with Mary implied an undertaking to be responsible to any child resulting from their relationship. This obligation seems to fall within the category of fidelity. Whatever label is attached to the duty, it clearly exists. Mary's obstinacy made it impossible for him to care for the child and stay with Corporation.

Jim also had a duty to Mary to maintain the marriage. The fact that Mary placed her career above Jim's promise to Corporation does not necessarily relieve Jim of his duty to keep the marriage intact. This duty comes under the heading of fidelity. There is also the pragmatic consideration that Mary's career opportunity is critical to her, whereas Jim's employment by Corporation is of minor significance to Corporation when viewed in isolation. There is, of course, the damage that is done to the relationship of trust between Corporation and employees like Jim when an event of this nature occurs.

It seems that despite the strong presumption that promises should be kept, Jim's conduct is justifiable. The moral duty to Corporation is outweighed by Jim's moral duty to the child and to maintain the marriage. Once again, others may disagree.

It is apparent that the resolution of moral conflicts, or dilemmas, involves weighing considerations that do not lend themselves to precise measurement, to understate the problem. Vague notions of utility are involved, as well as cultural and social values and moral intuitions. Assessments of utility are concerned with both the immediate impact among the parties involved and the social impact resulting from the universalization of the conduct.[17]

THE JUDGE AND THE IMMORAL LAW

It is useful to introduce the subject of the morality of lawyers' behavior with a brief discussion of the moral aspects of the behavior of judges. Assume that the criminal law provides that a property owner is guilty of a felony if he knowingly permits certain illegal drugs to be sold on his property. In an atmosphere of a war against drugs, a draconian mandatory minimum sentence of five years' imprisonment for the crime has been legislated. Grandmother has been raising in her home three teenaged grandsons whose father is unknown and whose mother is an alcoholic and a drifter. One of the grandsons is into drugs and conducts sales in the house. Grandmother works every day as a cleaning woman and has remonstrated with the delinquent grandson persistently to get out of drugs. The district attorney decided to clean up the street, which has a good deal of drug traffic, and successfully prosecutes, among others, the teenager and Grandmother. Grandmother has no prior criminal record. The judge sentences Grandmother to a five-year term, the mandatory minimum sentence. She may be released on probation in three years.

The judge believes that the law requiring a minimum sentence of this severity for a property owner is unconscionable and immoral in its application to certain defendants such as Grandmother, because the harm inflicted upon Grandmother is grossly disproportionate to the wrong that she has committed. He believes that she should receive a sentence of one year and immediate probation. Nevertheless he imposes the sentence as required by law.

Viewed independently of certain contextual circumstances, it appears that the judge has participated in the commission of what he believes to be an immoral act. But the judge has satisfied himself that the value of the legal system, which requires the sentence, outweighs the prima facie immorality of the sentence in the moral scales.

The criminal law is determined by the legislature. The executive branch of government in the person of the local district attorney has the discretionary authority to prosecute for criminal conduct. The judicial branch in the person of the jury determines guilt. The judge imposed the sentence as set forth in the legislation. Ordinarily the judge has broad discretion in sentencing and the use of probation to allow the convicted person to go free, but not in this case. The legislature, the district attorney, the jury, and the judge have their respective roles to play in the administration of criminal justice, and the system cannot function unless each performs its role.

Under the law the judge cannot choose not to hear the case; nor can he choose not to impose the sentence if there is a jury verdict of guilt. If he chooses not to hear the case that the district attorney has decided to prosecute, or not to impose the statutory minimum sentence, he is in defiance of the law, and the criminal justice system breaks down. The only means of avoidance available to the judge is to resign his position. If resignation is generalized—that is, if every judge resigns rather than impose a specified sentence–the system fails to function.

Because of the value of the system, the judge may conclude that the imposition of the mandatory minimum sentence is morally justifiable. He believes that the criminal justice system is fundamentally just, however flawed it may be, as in this case. The proper functioning of the system requires him to continue as a judge and to impose the sentence. The proper functioning of the criminal justice system is a social good that outweighs the immorality of Grandmother's sentence in the moral scales. The morality based on the performance of a special role in society is sometimes referred to as "role morality."[18] This will be discussed in more detail in the next section, which deals with the special role of the lawyer.

It should be noted that the district attorney is able to deal with the moral dilemma differently from the judge. The district attorney has the discretion not to prosecute a person who she believes has committed a crime. In this circumstance the district attorney may decide not to prosecute Grandmother on moral grounds because of the draconian nature of the required sentence.

If Grandmother is prosecuted, the jury is instructed by the judge that it must render a verdict of guilty if it concludes beyond a reasonable doubt that she has committed the crime. The jury makes its decision in secret, and its verdict is not subject to any requirement of explanation. The jury may believe that Grandmother is guilty beyond a reasonable doubt but render a verdict of acquittal because it believes that conviction is morally wrong or that she is entitled to mercy. It is extralegal conduct, but the system permits it. The law does not explicitly recognize that the jury is empowered to dispense morality or mercy rather than law, but all participants in the legal system are aware that juries sometimes decide in that fashion.[19]

THE ROLE MORALITY OF THE LAWYER

For the purpose of analyzing the justification for the behavior of lawyers that on its face appears to be immoral, it is necessary to categorize such behavior. First, there is the representation of the client who pursues an objective that is legal but immoral. Second, regardless of whether the client's objective is good, bad, or indifferent, there are the means or tactics used by the lawyer in the course of representation that are professionally permissible or obligatory but which deceive or harm others or impede justice. The analyses of these categories of behavior involve different considerations, and each category will be discussed separately. In this chapter we shall consider the representation of the client who pursues an immoral but legal objective; in Chapter 3 we shall consider the morality of certain means and tactics employed by the lawyer in pursuit of the client's legal objective, whether good, bad, or indifferent.

Several of the examples in Chapter 1 involved the representation of clients whose objectives were legal but of questionable morality. Example 19 concerned the building contractor who deliberately breached his contract and then successfully pleaded the two-year statute of limitations for breach of contract when the other party sued shortly after the two-year period had expired. Example 20 concerned the television producer who produces programs containing violence, sadism, and promiscuous sex. Example 21 concerned the gambling entrepreneur. Example 22 concerned a Nazi group that wished to conduct a parade in a predominantly Jewish area carrying signs advocating genocide.

All of these objectives are legal and do harm without justification. The law allows these harms to be done for various reasons: (1) The genocidal speech and the television trash are protected by the First Amendment; harmful speech is protected for fear that restricting speech of this nature may lead to restrictions upon controversial and unpopular speech that is worthy of protection. This is the "slippery slope" argument. (2) The statute of limitations exists to protect people who are not or may not be liable, from suits brought long after the event when it may be difficult to establish one's defense because memories are dim, witnesses may have left town or died, or evidence may have been lost or destroyed. The statute, however, is unconditional and sometimes protects those who are clearly and admittedly liable. The reasons for the unconditional nature of the statute are to encourage people to resolve disputes promptly and to avoid the expense of litigating in each instance the justification for the use of the statute. (3) The gambling casino is allowed probably because we have come to accept this vice as inevitable, so the community may as well derive the economic benefits and the taxes from the business.

If the legal conduct of the client is immoral, it follows that others who participate or assist in the conduct are morally culpable. The contention is, however, that the lawyer is not morally accountable because of the special nature of her role in the administration of the legal system. This form of moral justification is sometimes referred to as role morality. Its essence is that the role the individual is performing constitutes a sufficient justification for doing something that would otherwise be morally wrong to do. In the performance of the role, the lawyer may morally do something for her client that she cannot morally do for herself or for anyone other than her client.

In our system of freedom under law, legislators and judges are responsible for the making of law. Whatever its flaws, our system of law is fundamentally just. Each member of our society is entitled to avail himself of what the law allows. The law, however, is complex and often arcane. The citizen can avail himself of the law's opportunities only if he has the assistance of the expert on the subject, the lawyer. The lawyer is the citizen's guide through the legal thicket. If the lawyer's assistance is not available to him, the citizen is denied a vital aspect of his citizenship. The legal profession is essential to the effective functioning of our system of freedom under law.

The law permits immoral things to be done. Sometimes there is a good reason for it, as in the case of the misuse of First Amendment rights. Sometimes it is too much trouble to police the wrong, as in the case of the unjustified use of the statute of limitations. Sometimes we accept the inevitability of the vice, as in commercial gambling. Sometimes there is no adequate explanation for it, as in the case of forms of environmental degradation that are permitted. There is also a strand in our social thinking that, where feasible, moral decisions should be left to the individual. There is much to be said for this position, unless the immoral decision significantly harms others.

If the law allows a citizen to pursue an immoral objective, he is entitled to a lawyer to advise and guide him. The proper functioning of our system of law dictates this. In the moral scales, the good of the effective functioning of the fundamentally just system outweighs the moral wrong of the lawyer's participation in the pursuit of the objective. This is the essence of the role morality argument in defense of the lawyer's behavior.[20]

In moral reasoning, a prima facie wrong may be justified if the act achieves a good that is more significant than the harm done. Role morality is simply a specific form of the moral balancing process. This justification of the lawyer's role in legal but immoral activity is not accepted by some moral philosophers and members of the profession.[21] (Challenges to the morality of the lawyer's role are discussed later in this chapter.)

It should be emphasized that this reasoning makes it morally *permissible* for a lawyer to serve a client's immoral objective; the proponents of this position do not assert that it is morally *obligatory* for a lawyer to represent a client with such an objective. The lawyer is morally entitled not to represent such a client. Indeed the professional rules make it clear that the lawyer can decline clients, whether on moral grounds, on grounds of their inability to pay the lawyer's hourly rate, or on other grounds.[22] (The ramifications of this selectivity are also discussed later in this chapter.)

There are analogues to the role morality of the lawyer. We have already discussed the very compelling role morality of the judge. Another is the role of the parent in relation to her children. Richard Wasserstrom, a professor of philosophy as well as a lawyer, has described it:

> If parents were ever pressed to justify, as they very seldom are, why it is right
> that they do and should prefer the interests of their children over those of any or

all of the other children in the world, it would surely be on the ground that their role as the parents of these children requires (or at minimum allows) them to prefer their welfare and their interests over those of all other children.[23]

The differential treatment of children is, on its face, a violation of the duty of justice (equal treatment unless there is justification for differential treatment). The justification is the special role of the parent. Society is best served if parents tend to the needs of their children preferentially. Another justification is the implicit undertaking to care for the children whom one has brought into being; this undertaking is an example of the fundamental moral duty of fidelity.

Wasserstrom offers another analogue, that of the general in war:

> Suppose, for instance, a general is confronted with two ways to secure an objective. With one plan it can be accomplished by the probable loss of 2,000 of his own troops and 4,000 of the enemy's. With a different plan it can be accomplished with a probable loss of 1,000 of his own troops and 15,000 of the enemy's. With the first plan 6,000 persons will be killed; with the second one, 16,000 persons will be killed, but only half as many of his own. His role, the general would surely say, is to prefer the interests of his own troops over those of the enemy's and, therefore, the second plan is the right one for him to implement—even if many more persons will be killed than if the first plan is adopted. And the reasoning would not, I think, be different if the losses to the enemy included large numbers of civilians and noncombatants as well as enemy soldiers. The role of the general qua general is, very largely if not exclusively, to secure the greatest advantage for his side with the least net losses to that side.[24]

This analogy seems to require that the general's nation is engaged in a just war, for if it is not, the killing of the enemy cannot be justified. The killing, on its face, is a moral wrong; if it is done in the course of a just war, it may be morally justified. In addition, minimizing the losses to the general's forces at whatever cost to the enemy is also justified.

Once again, what is referred to as role morality is simply a form of justification for a prima facie wrong that serves a good purpose that outweighs the wrong on the moral scales.

CLIENT AUTONOMY AS MORAL JUSTIFICATION

Stephen Pepper, a professor of law, has offered a moral justification for the lawyer's participation in the client's legal but immoral objective that is different from the justification described above. The essence of Pepper's theory is the moral value of aiding the client's autonomy.[25]

Pepper's reasoning begins with the premise that law is a public good. Society, through its "lawmakers"—legislatures, courts, and administrative agencies—has created mechanisms to enable the private attainment of individual goals and to resolve conflicts. His second premise is that our system of freedom under law is founded upon individual autonomy as a social and moral good. We believe that choice is better than constraint, that each person should be entitled to make her own choices rather than to have them made for her. Our legal system accommodates individual autonomy by leaving a great deal of room for private choice.

The law makes intolerable conduct unlawful; that, Pepper states,

> sets a floor below which one cannot go, but leaves as much room as possible above that floor for individual decision making. It may be morally wrong to manufacture or distribute cigarettes or alcohol, or to disinherit one's children for marrying outside the faith, but the generality of such decisions are left in the private realm. Diversity and autonomy are preferred over "right" or "good" conduct.[26]

Note that Pepper asserts that above the floor set by the law, the moral value of autonomy outweighs in the moral scales the moral wrong that may be done in the exercise of the autonomy. He states that our system implicitly recognizes this.

The exercise of autonomy in our complex and regulated society often requires access to the law, which is generally available only through a lawyer. It is wrong for the lawyer to interpose her moral judgment to prevent the exercise of the client's autonomy. If such interposition were generalized, it would establish a moral oligarchy of lawyers at the expense of client autonomy.

Pepper's theory does not merely allow the lawyer to participate in the client's immoral objective, it requires her to do so. To decline the representation on moral grounds interferes with the autonomy of the client. This position is to be distinguished from the more conventional role morality justification described above, which permits, but does not require, such representation. However, Pepper recognizes that there may be circumstances so repugnant to the lawyer's sense of right and wrong that she may properly decline the representation. He refers to this as "conscientious objection."

Pepper recognizes that access to the legal profession is limited by the ability of the client to pay. Although the free market for legal services impairs autonomy, he denies that this vitiates his position that the lawyer must disregard the morality of the client's objective. If the lawyer declines representation for moral reasons, unavailability of access is aggravated; access then may be denied in circumstances in which the client can pay the fee. If the lawyer serves as a moral constraint, unavailability of access is compounded. The free market for legal services presents serious problems of a moral nature, but that is an entirely different matter from blocking access based on the lawyer's moral view.[27]

Pepper's moral theory is an interesting one. It locates moral justification for the lawyer's behavior in the client's autonomy, rather than in the proper functioning of the system. The proper functioning of the system is, of course, integral to this theory, but it is not the locus of the moral justification. Although he does not say so explicitly, it must be assumed that the legal system is fundamentally just; the exercise of autonomy within a fundamentally unjust legal system could not be a significant moral value.

Pepper's view that individual autonomy is a basic moral value is clearly supportable. We have described the fundamental components of morality as avoiding harm, helping others, keeping promises, not lying, and giving each what he is due. At the center of the concept of morality is the dignity, the value, the freedom, the self-determination, of the human being. The human being is not to be harmed or lied to or discriminated against, and the promises that are made to a human being are to be kept. If these duties are performed by others including the state, the individual will be free and self-determining and have dignity. If morality imposes such duties, it follows that the individual has the moral right to freedom, self-determination, and dignity. Autonomy is a moral value that is a function of the fundamental moral constraints.

Finally, Pepper makes reference to the opportunity that the lawyer has to inform the client of her view that the client's objective is morally tainted.[28] The client, of course, may have given the matter considerable thought and have justified his proposed course of conduct in his own mind. Both parties may be educated by a "moral conversation."[29] Under the conventional role morality justification and Pepper's "autonomy" justification for lawyer behavior, raising the moral issue is, of course, permissible, but there is no suggestion that it is a condition of the justification for the lawyer's participation in the immoral conduct. It seems that if a lawyer believes the client's objective is morally wrong, raising the question should be a condition of the justification of the representation.

The Response to
the Lawyer's Role Morality

The rationales for the participation of the lawyer in the accomplishment of the client's immoral objective are not, of course, universally accepted. First, we shall deal with responses to the conventional role morality justification that the proper functioning of the legal system requires that the lawyer disregard her moral concerns.

Richard Wasserstrom has expressed doubts about the lawyer's role morality and its conventional systemic justification:

[A]ll of the arguments that support the role-differentiated amorality of the lawyer on institutional grounds can succeed only if the enormous degree of trust and confidence in the institutions themselves is itself justified. If the institutions work well and fairly, there may be good sense to deferring important moral concerns and criticisms to another time and place, to the level of institutional criticism and assessment. But the less certain we are entitled to be of either the rightness or the self-corrective nature of the larger institutions of which the professional is a part, the less apparent it is that we should encourage the professional to avoid direct engagement with the moral issues as they arise. And we are, today, I believe, certainly entitled to be quite skeptical both of the fairness and of the capacity for self-correction of our larger institutional mechanisms, including the legal system. To the degree to which the institutional rules and practices are unjust, unwise or undesirable, to that same degree is the case for the role-differentiated behavior of the lawyer weakened if not destroyed.[30]

In sum, if the legal system is fundamentally flawed, it follows that there is no justification for the representation of the client who is pursuing a legal but immoral objective.

Wasserstrom's reference to the flawed system is unspecific. Others have cited the free-market nature of lawyers' services. Access to lawyers' services is determined by the citizens' ability to pay. Some can't afford the services at all. For those who can, the more they can afford to pay, the better the services they can obtain. Highly skilled legal services are very expensive. The system of law may be just in the abstract, but in practice the imbalance of lawyers' services compromises the ideal. In other words, the system provides the wealthy a good deal more "justice" than it does the middle class and the poor. This argument is a significant challenge to the position that the fundamentally just system justifies the lawyer's assistance in the achievement of the legal but immoral objective of the client.[31]

There is also the related matter of the way lawyers are permitted or required to practice their profession. There are many tactics and practices employed by lawyers, illustrated in Chapter 1, that have the effect of impeding the achievement of the result called for under the law. An argument founded on systemic justice is significantly challenged by the profession's use of means that are designed to undermine it.[32]

Finally, the legal system is premised upon classical liberal principles of private property, freedom of contract, and economic competition. There are those who believe that these principles are themselves inherently unfair or at least produce substantial injustice. To the extent that one denies the social or moral value of classical liberal principles and the uneven distribution of wealth that results, the argument for the role morality of the lawyer is correspondingly diminished.

Even if one assumes that the system is fundamentally just, there is the criticism of the conventional role morality justification that the functioning of the system is not likely to be adversely affected by the lawyer's refusal to represent the client in his pursuit of the immoral objective. If a lawyer declines the representation on moral grounds, there are undoubtedly other lawyers who will accept the representation because they do not share the first lawyer's view that the objective is immoral or because they do not consider that moral considerations have any bearing upon the decision to represent the client.[33]

In this context there are two possible situations in which the rejection of representation on moral grounds could result in the denial of the client's access to the opportunities afforded by the law. One is the situation in which the client's objective is so obnoxious that no lawyer, even one who ordinarily disregards moral concerns, will accept the representation. Alan Goldman, a moral philosopher, states that in this case "the immorality of the client's purpose outweighs the value of allowing him the autonomy of pursuing it."[34] In other words, in this instance the functioning of the system is not of paramount importance; indeed, it is morally preferable in this circumstance that it does not function.

It is not clear that this is a satisfactory response to the conventional justification. It may be that in this extraordinary and unlikely situation the morally sensitive lawyer should reconsider her refusal of representation.

Goldman posits another situation in which, for geographical reasons, a particular lawyer is the only one available who possesses the expertise required by the client, and that lawyer refuses the representation because she finds the client's objective immoral. Goldman states that the lawyer should search her soul to be certain that the immorality of the objective outweighs the wrong of the denial of access to the law, and if she so concludes, the rejection is the right course.[35] However, it is not convincing that in a fundamentally just system this is the proper response.

It is interesting that some moral philosophers who are skeptical of the validity of the conventional role morality justification for the behavior of lawyers make an exception for the lawyer who represents the criminal defendant who she knows is guilty. Wasserstrom, for example, has this to say about the moral distinction between criminal defense and other forms of representation:

> I do believe that the amoral behavior of the *criminal* defense lawyer is justifiable. But I think that jurisdiction depends at least as much upon the special needs of an accused as upon any more general defense of a lawyer's role-differentiated behavior. . . . Because a deprivation of liberty is so serious, because the prosecutorial resources of the state are so vast, and because, perhaps, of a serious skepticism about the rightness of punishment even where wrongdoing has occurred, it is easy to accept the view that it makes sense to charge the defense counsel with the job of making the best possible case for the accused—without regard, so to speak, for the merits. This coupled with the fact that it is an adversarial proceeding succeeds, I think, in justifying the amorality of the criminal defense counsel. But this does not, however, justify a comparable perspec-

tive on the part of lawyers generally. Once we leave the peculiar situation of the criminal defense lawyer, I think it quite likely that the role-differentiated amorality of the lawyer is almost certainly excessive and at times inappropriate. That is to say, this special case to one side, I am inclined to think that we might all be better served if lawyers were to see themselves less as subject to role-differentiated behavior and more as subject to the demands of the moral point of view.[36]

David Luban, another moral philosopher who rejects generally the role morality justification for lawyer behavior, justifies criminal defense in all circumstances:

[C]riminal defense is a very special case in which the zealous advocate serves atypical social goals. The point is one of political theory. The goal of zealous advocacy in criminal defense is to curtail the power of the state over its citizens. We want to handicap the state in its power even legitimately to punish us. And so the adversary system is justified, not because it is a good way of achieving justice, but because it is a good way of hobbling the government and we have political reasons for wanting this. The argument, in other words, does not claim that the adversary system is the best way of obtaining justice. It claims just the opposite, that it is the best way of impeding justice in the name of more fundamental political ends, namely keeping the government's hands off people. Nothing, of course, is wrong with that; indeed, I believe that Brougham's imperative may well hold in criminal defense. My point is merely that criminal defense is an exceptional part of the legal system, one that aims at protection rather than justice.[37]

The rationale offered to justify the universal morality of criminal defense representation by those who oppose the role morality principle for lawyers in the civil context reflects hostility to the criminal justice system. The bias is explicit. The criminal justice system is assumed to be inherently unfair; it follows that representation of the criminal defendant is always right and moral. That may be something of an oversimplification, but it captures the essence of the position.

THE RESPONSE TO THE
CLIENT AUTONOMY JUSTIFICATION

Now we will deal with the response to Stephen Pepper's justification of the lawyer's role. Pepper's position is that the value of individual autonomy with respect to legal conduct that is immoral outweighs, in the moral scales, the immorality of the conduct. As a society we have left decisions in the realm of the legal to the judgment of the individual. Consequently the lawyer acts morally when she assists the client in his legal but immoral conduct. On the other hand, conduct that is intolerable is made illegal and is removed from the realm of individual autonomy.

Luban contests Pepper's reasoning on two levels. First, although autonomy with respect to decisions with moral significance is an important value, it is a different moral consideration from the nature of the exercise of that autonomy. In other words, it is morally valuable that the individual should have the freedom to decide whether or not to exercise his legal right to pursue an immoral objective, but the decision to pursue the objective is nevertheless immoral.[38] This reasoning presents a fundamental challenge to Pepper's theory. Pepper asserts that as a society we have placed a higher value on autonomy than on "good" conduct.

Even if the moral value of autonomy trumps the immorality of the chosen objective, as Pepper maintains, Luban contends that Pepper's distinction between the nature of what is legally permissible and the nature of what is illegal and intolerable is not sound. Luban's point is that often conduct that is legal is worse than conduct that is illegal. For example, smuggling a bottle of whiskey into this country is a crime, but preaching genocide is legal. Luban states:

> There are many reasons for not prohibiting conduct besides the reason that we don't think it's bad enough to take it out of people's hands. We should not put into effect prohibitions that are unenforceable, or that are enforceable only at enormous cost, or through unacceptably or disproportionately invasive means. We should not prohibit immoral conduct if it would be too difficult to specify the conduct, or if the laws would of necessity be vague or either over- or underinclusive, or if enforcement would destroy our liberties.[39]

If conduct that is legal is sometimes more reprehensible than conduct that is illegal, Pepper's argument for the value of autonomy within the realm of the legal is weakened. Pepper recognizes that this may sometimes be the case but maintains that there is no justification for the interposition of the lawyer's moral judgment even in this instance. There is an implicit theme in Pepper's thinking of skepticism concerning moral judgment; who is to say what is moral and what is not? Why should the lawyer's judgment be substituted for that of the client, even in this circumstance? The less confidence there is in the objectivity of moral judgment, the greater the value that is placed on autonomy.

TWO SPECIAL SITUATIONS: BREACH OF CONTRACT AND SEEKING ACQUITTAL FOR THE RAPE-MURDERER

Two of the examples in Chapter 1 involving the lawyer's participation in the attainment of the client's immoral objective require particular analysis. The first is Example 7, in which the client, Manufacturer, wants to "break" its long-term contract with Supplier because Manufacturer has located a source of substitute materials that are less expensive than the materials it contracted to purchase from Supplier. The lawyer counsels and assists her client concerning the breach of contract. The second is Example 23, in which the lawyer is seeking an acquittal for his client, a rape-murderer, who admits to the lawyer that he committed the crime.

Bear in mind that here we are concerned primarily with the justification for the lawyer's participation in the achievement of the legal but immoral objective of the client. The willful breach of contract explored in Example 7, on the other hand, is both illegal and immoral. It is illegal because the breach gives the nonbreaching party the right to sue for damages or, in some unusual instances, for a court order requiring the breaching party to specifically perform its contractual obligation. By definition, legal liability is the consequence of the violation of law.

A contract is a promise. The willful failure to perform a promise is a violation of a fundamental moral duty. Telling the truth and keeping promises are the substance of the moral duty of fidelity.

One may make a sophistic argument that the failure to perform the contractual promise is not illegal or immoral because the promise made is that the promisor—that is, the person who makes the promise—will do what he says he will do or, if he does not do it, he will pay the promisee whatever losses he incurs.[40] If the contract explicitly stated that the promise was for performance in this alternative form, the conclusion would be correct. But contracts virtually never provide for such alternative performance. The promisee expects that the promisor will do what he said he would do and relies on that. When it is not done, there are various disruptive and harmful consequences, some of which are monetarily quantifiable and some of which are not; the latter make the question of damages very problematic.[41]

Let us consider an analogy to the sophistic theory that the promise is alternatively to perform or pay damages and that the failure to perform is neither illegal nor immoral. The law provides that a person is liable for damages if he negligently (or deliberately) injures another or his property. This is known as a tort. Injury caused negligently or deliberately is illegal. Using the sophistry mentioned in connection with the breach of contract, it may be said that one is entitled to negligently or deliberately injure another legally as long as one compensates the victim for the injury. There is no immorality because by compensating the victim the negligent party has avoided inflicting any harm.[42] Clearly the victim of the injury and the victim of the breach of contract view the matter differently. It cannot be seriously maintained that the breach of contract and the negligent or willful harm are not illegal and immoral.

A lawyer is forbidden to counsel or assist a client in fraudulent or criminal conduct. The breach of contract does not involve fraud and is not a crime. It is, however, illegal, but the professional rules in most states permit the lawyer to counsel and assist the client in illegal conduct other than fraud and crime. What is the moral justification for the lawyer's participation in achieving a client's immoral objective that is also outside the law? The role morality and autonomy justifications presuppose that the client's conduct is within the law in a fundamentally just system of law. If the client's immoral objective is outside the law, there is no systemic justification for the lawyer's participation. The lawyer's conduct is unqualifiedly immoral. It is remarkable that the professional rules permit the lawyer to counsel the client to engage in violations of civil law and to assist the client in such violation.

Counseling and assisting the client in the breach of contract is, of course, very different from representing the client after he has committed the breach. The lawyer who represents the client in negotiations for settlement after the breach, or in litigation for breach of contract, is assisting the client in resolving a past wrong in accordance with the law.

Now let us look at the question of the lawyer's efforts to obtain an acquittal for the admittedly guilty rape-murderer described in Example 23. Is the lawyer participating in the achievement of the immoral objective of avoiding punishment for his client? If one accepts that punishment for crime is morally justified, then it follows that participating in an effort to avoid punishment for the guilty is prima facie immoral. Such prima facie immorality, however, may be justified on the systemic ground that the law requires that the state prove beyond a reasonable doubt that the defendant committed the crime. The defendant is constitutionally entitled not to testify. The lawyer's representation provides his client with what the law allows him.

There is another morally justificatory aspect to consider. The law imposes upon the state the extraordinary standard that the defendant's guilt must be established beyond a reasonable doubt. In contrast, the standard in the civil suit is that the plaintiff must establish that it is more likely than not that his account of the facts is correct. It is accepted that the criminal standard results in acquittals for many guilty criminal defendants. The system allows this to happen to assure that the innocent are not convicted. The lawyer's representation of the guilty defendant serves the broader societal purpose of avoiding the appalling result of the conviction of the innocent. In the service of this objective the lawyer is absolved from any personal responsibility for the representation of the guilty.

Notes

1. Geoffrey F. Warnock, The Object of Morality 16, 26 (Methuen, 1971).
2. *Id.* at 80–87.

3. See Alan Donagan, The Theory of Morality 76–100 (Chicago, 1977); William K. Frankena, Ethics 43–55 (Prentice-Hall, 2d ed., 1973); Bernard Gert, Morality 96–159 (Oxford, 1988); Anthony Quinton, Utilitarian Ethics 69 (St. Martin's, 1973); W. D. Ross, The Right and the Good 21 (Hackett, 1988); Peter F. Strawson, Freedom and Resentment 38 (Methuen, 1974).

4. See James Rachels, The Elements of Moral Philosophy 90–116 (McGraw-Hill, 2d ed., 1993); Tom L. Beauchamp and James F. Childress, Principles of Biomedical Ethics 26–36 (Oxford, 3d ed., 1989); John J.C. Smart and Bernard A. Williams, Utilitarianism: For and Against (University Press, 1973). The philosophical origins of utilitarianism are to be found in Jeremy Bentham's *Principles of Morals and Legislation,* published in The Utilitarians (Anchor Books, 1973), and in John Stuart Mill's Utilitarianism, also published in The Utilitarians (Anchor Books, 1973).

5. W. D. Ross, The Right and the Good 29 (Hackett, 1988). For discussions of intuitionism, see Alan Donagan, The Theory of Morality 22 (Chicago, 1977); William K. Frankena, Ethics 102–105 (Prentice-Hall, 2d ed., 1973); Tom Regan, The Case for Animal Rights 133 (California, 1983); John Rawls, A Theory of Justice 34 (Harvard, 1971).

6. John Rawls, A Theory of Justice vii–viii (Harvard, 1971).

7. Immanuel Kant, Critique of Practical Reason 346–350 (Lewis White Beck ed. and trans., University of Chicago Press, 1949); Immanuel Kant, Groundwork of the Metaphysics of Morals 84–87 (H. J. Paton ed. and trans., Hutchinson, 1967).

8. James Rachels, The Elements of Moral Philosophy 148 (McGraw-Hill, 2d ed., 1993).

9. Sissela Bok, Lying 42–46 (Vintage, 1978); Tom Beauchamp and James F. Childress, Principles of Biomedical Ethics 37 (Oxford, 3d ed., 1989).

10. See Martin P. Golding, Philosophy of Law 32 (Prentice-Hall, 1975); James Rachels, The Elements of Moral Philosophy 50 (McGraw-Hill, 2d ed., 1993).

11. Joseph F. Fletcher, Situation Ethics (Westminster, 1966).

12. Sissela Bok, Lying xix (Vintage, 1978).

13. For an excellent discussion of and source for biomedical ethics, see Tom L. Beauchamp and James F. Childress, Principles of Biomedical Ethics (Oxford, 3d ed., 1989). See also John D. Arras and Nancy K. Rhoden, Ethical Issues in Modern Medicine, Appendix: Resources in Bioethics (Mayfield, 3d ed., 1989); Barry R. Furrow, Sandra H. Johnson, Timothy S. Jost, and Robert L. Schwartz, Bioethics (West, 1991).

14. William K. Frankena, Ethics 55–56 (Prentice-Hall, 2d ed., 1973); Bernard Gert, Morality 96–159 (Oxford, 1988); Robert M. Hare, Moral Thinking 25–64 (Clarendon, 1981); David Lyons, Ethics and the Rule of Law 81, 84, 106 (Cambridge, 1984); W. D. Ross, The Right and the Good 28–42 (Hackett, 1988); James D. Wallace, Moral Behavior and Moral Conflict 78–95 (Cornell, 1988). See generally, Sissela Bok, Lying (Vintage, 1978); Tom L. Beauchamp and James F. Childress, Principles of Biomedical Ethics (Oxford, 3d ed., 1989).

15. John Rawls, A Theory of Justice 83 (Harvard, 1971).

16. *Id.* at 114.

17. Substantial portions of the preceding material in this Chapter 2 appeared in an article by this author in 66 *Notre Dame Law Review* 1025, at 1034-38 (1991), entitled Teaching Moral Analysis in Law School. Copyright by Notre Dame Law Review, University of Notre Dame. Reproduced with permission.

18. For a somewhat different analysis of the role morality of the judge, see Alan H. Goldman, The Moral Foundations of Professional Ethics 38–49 (Rowman & Littlefield, 1980).

19. This conduct is often referred to as jury "nullification." It has been said that the jury has the "power" to nullify, but not the "right" to do so. Two hundred years ago it was widely accepted that the jury had the "right" to nullify, but since the middle of the nineteenth century this has not been part of our jurisprudence except for Maryland and Indiana which recognize it as a proper function of the jury. For a thorough discussion of the history and policy of this issue, see Alan W. Scheflin, Jury Nullification: The Right to Say No, 45 *Southern California Law Review* 168 (1972). See also Paul Butler, Racially Based Jury Nullification: Black Power in the Criminal Justice System, 105 *Yale Law Journal* 677 (1995); Alan W. Scheflin and Jon M. Van dyke, Merciful Juries: The Resilience of Jury Nullification, 48 *Washington & Lee Law Review* 165 (1991); Gary J. Simson, Jury Nullification in the American System: A Skeptical View, 54 *Texas Law Review* 488 (1976).

20. Role morality of lawyers is clearly expounded, although not approved, in Richard Wasserstrom, Lawyers as Professionals: Some Moral Issues, 5 *Human Rights* 1 (1975); and Richard Wasserstrom, *Roles and Morality,* in The Good Lawyer 25 (D. Luban ed., Rowman and Allanheld, 1984). See also Alan Donagan, *Justifying Legal Practice in the Adversary System,* in The Good Lawyer 123 (D. Luban ed., Rowman & Allanheld, 1984); Monroe H. Freedman, Understanding Lawyers' Ethics 44–47 (Matthew Bender, 1990); Charles Fried, The Lawyer as Friend: The Moral Foundations of the Lawyer-Client Relation, 85 *Yale Law Journal* 1060 (1976).

21. See Alan H. Goldman, The Moral Foundations of Professional Ethics 106–137 (Rowman & Littlefield, 1980); David Luban, Lawyers and Justice 148–174 (Princeton, 1988); David Luban, *The Adversary System Excuse,* in The Good Lawyer 83 (D. Luban ed., Rowman & Allanheld, 1984).

22. The rules contain no provision obligating a lawyer to represent a client. Indeed, after the lawyer has accepted a client, the lawyer is free to terminate the representation as long as this can be done without injury to the client's interest. Model Rule 1.16.

23. Richard Wasserstrom, *Roles and Morality,* in The Good Lawyer 26 (D. Luban ed., Rowman and Allenheld, 1984).

24. *Id.* at 27.

25. Stephen L. Pepper, The Lawyer's Amoral Ethical Role: A Defense, a Problem, and Some Possibilities, 1986 *American Bar Foundation Research Journal* 613.

26. *Id.* at 617.

27. *Id.* at 619.

28. *Id.* at 630.

29. See Thomas L. Shaffer, On Being a Christian and a Lawyer 21 (Brigham Young, 1981).

30. Richard Wasserstrom, Lawyers as Professionals: Some Moral Issues, 5 *Human Rights* 12 (1975). Permission to reprint granted by the American Bar Association, the Section of Individual Rights and Responsibilities, and Southern Methodist University.

31. Alan H. Goldman, The Moral Foundations of Professional Ethics 123 (Rowman & Littlefield, 1980).

32. David Luban, *The Adversary Excuse,* in The Good Lawyer 83, 94 (D. Luban ed., Rowman & Allenheld, 1984); Alan H. Goldman, The Moral Foundations of Professional Ethics 114 (Rowman & Littlefield, 1980).

33. Alan H. Goldman, The Moral Foundations of Professional Ethics 130 (Rowman & Littlefield, 1980).

34. *Id.* at 132.

35. *Id.* at 130.

36. Richard Wasserstrom, Lawyers as Professionals: Some Moral Issues, 5 *Human Rights* 12 (1975). Permission to reprint granted by the American Bar Association, the Section of Individual Rights and Responsibilities, and Southern Methodist University.

37. David Luban, *The Adversary System Excuse,* in The Good Lawyer 92 (D. Luban ed., Rowman & Allenheld, 1984).

38. David Luban, The Lysistration Prerogative: A Response to Stephen Pepper, 1986 *American Bar Foundation Research Journal* 637.

39. *Id.* at 640.

40. This view originated with Oliver Wendell Holmes, who stated, "The duty to keep a contract at common law means a prediction that you must pay damages if you do not keep it—and nothing more." The Path of the Law, 10 *Harvard Law Review* 457, 462 (1897). This is a widely, but not universally, held view among academics and practitioners today. It is safe to say that fifty years ago most would attribute normative significance to the contractual promise. Holmes was a man far ahead of his time.

The moralist position is expounded in Charles Fried, Contract as Promise (Harvard, 1981).

41. Economic analysts of law contend that a breach of contract is socially desirable if it results in the increased efficiency in the use of the resources that are the subject of the contract. Seller contracts with First Buyer for the sale of specific goods. Before Seller delivers he discovers Second Buyer who is willing to pay more for the goods. Second Buyer's higher offer indicates that the goods have a greater usefulness in his hands than they would in the hands of First Buyer. The sale to Second Buyer would, therefore, be an efficient use of these goods. Seller breaches his contract with First Buyer by selling to Second Buyer, compensates First Buyer for any damages he has suffered, and pockets the difference between damages to First Buyer and his profit on the sale to Second Buyer. As the theory goes, nobody is hurt and society has benefited because the property is being put to its most valuable use.

This reasoning has some holes in it. It assumes that damages can be precisely and readily determined. This is never the case as a practical matter. Damages must be determined by negotiation, which is burdensome and costs money. In addition, there are inconveniences and psychological harms imposed on the First Buyer that are neither quantifiable nor compensable. Furthermore, if the payment of damages to First Buyer is functionally equivalent to performance of the contract by Seller, why doesn't Seller simply negotiate a release from his contract with First Buyer, which provides for the payment of damages? There is the further objection that it is intuitively just that First Buyer should receive the benefit of the higher price that Second Buyer is willing to pay. See E. Allan Farnsworth, Contract, Vol. III, § 12.3 (Little, Brown, 1990).

42. The conventional amoral economic analysis of tort liability is not as extreme or as offensive as this, but it does bear a resemblance. Liability for harm caused by negligence is not viewed as having normative behavioral significance; liability is simply a cost of such behavior. See Guido Calabresi, *Torts—The Law of the Mixed Society*, in American Law: The Third Century 108–110 (B. Schwartz ed., New York University, 1976).

3

The Morality of the Means

We now move from considering the justification for the lawyer's representation of the client whose objective is legal but immoral, to considering the justification for the *means* employed by lawyers in their representation of the client, whether the objective is good, bad, or indifferent. The professional rules permit the lawyer to accept or decline representation, but once representation has been accepted, the lawyer becomes a fiduciary of the client for the purpose of achieving the client's objective. The lawyer owes her client exclusive and zealous dedication to his interest in order to obtain for him all that the law allows—and, as pointed out in some of the examples in Chapter 1, sometimes more than the law allows.

There is a further distinction between the subject matter of Chapter 2 and the subject matter of this chapter. In Chapter 2 we were concerned with the question of whether the lawyer's participation in the client's immoral objective was morally permissible for the lawyer. The means described in many of the examples in Chapter 1 harm people, deceive people, or impede justice; such means are at least prima facie immoral, although they are legal. The systemic reasoning that purports to justify the behavior of lawyers with respect to legal but immoral objectives applies equally to the behavior of lawyers with respect to means that are legal but immoral. The means are as much a part of the fundamentally just legal system as the objectives. The focus in this chapter, however, is not on the morality of the lawyer's personal behavior, but rather on the moral justification of the harmful or deceptive or obstructive means themselves. Such means are prima facie immoral; in order to be morally justified, such means must serve the purpose of affording the client what he is entitled to under the law in our fundamentally just legal system, or they must provide some other social or moral value that outweighs their prima facie immorality in the moral scales.

There is another important point to keep in mind during our discussion of means. Whereas the objectives that may be pursued under the law are determined or controlled by the legislative branch of government, the means that are permissible in the practice of law are usually determined by the courts. The means are the province of the profession. The legislature governs public policy, but the profession controls the means employed by lawyers.[1]

Many of the examples in Chapter 1 focus on the preparation for or anticipation of trial, the settlement outside of court, or the trial itself. The following brief description and assessment of the nature of our adversarial style of litigation will provide background and perspective for the moral analysis of many of the specific tactics and practices that are discussed in this chapter.

LITIGATION AS FACT-FINDING

Litigation is the process for discovering the facts of a dispute, to which the law is applied to effect a just resolution. Confrontation of zealously adversarial attorneys is the means employed to provide the impartial fact-finder (judge or jury, depending on the nature of the trial) with what he or they need to determine what has happened. Whatever evidence is presented by one adversary, the other attempts to refute or discredit. This quest for truth is, however, qualified by other values. Truth is impeded by the Constitutional principle that a person may not be compelled to testify against himself with respect to a criminal matter (the privilege against self-incrimination).[2] The most common example is that of the criminal defendant who may or may not testify at his trial, as he chooses. It is a uniquely painful indignity to be involuntarily subjected to incriminatory examination by the prosecution. The pursuit of truth is compromised in the interest of human dignity.

Truth is impeded by the attorney-client privilege, which forbids the attorney from testifying about communications from his client.[3] To represent the client adequately the lawyer must obtain all relevant information from the client. To do this effectively there must be the assurance that the lawyer will not voluntarily disclose or be compelled to disclose. The information may be very personal or damaging to the client. There is the parallel physician-patient privilege that protects medical information from disclosure by the physician. Certain private communications to a clergyman and certain communications by one spouse to the other are also privileged from disclosure in court.[4] The value of the pursuit of truth in the courts is subordinated to the freedom of communication and the need for privacy in these contexts. There is also the Constitutional protection against unreasonable searches of a person or a person's property by public authorities; if these Constitutional rights are violated, the evidence obtained as a result of the violation is usually not admissible in court.[5] Once again, the value of privacy prevails over truth in the courtroom.

The various privileges and exclusions aside, our style of litigation is indeed a unique method for determining the truth. Each lawyer is required to use his best efforts to convince the fact-finder that the facts of the dispute are such as to support a legal result favorable to his client, whether or not the lawyer believes that the facts support his client's position. The lawyer may present evidence in support of his client's position that he doubts is true, as long as he does not know it is false. Each lawyer is required not to disclose voluntarily the existence of evidence known to him that supports his adversary's position. Each lawyer is required to use his best efforts to discredit the evidence presented by the adversary, whether or not he believes such evidence is true; this may be accomplished by means of cross-examination of an adversary's witness to impeach the credibility of her testimony or by the presentation of other evidence. The basic constraints upon the lawyer's conduct are that he must not lie or affirmatively present testimony or other evidence that he knows to be false.

Some years ago when he was a federal trial court judge, Marvin Frankel described the relationship between truth and trial practice:

> We proclaim to each other and to the world that the clash of adversaries is a powerful means for hammering out the truth. Sometimes, less guardedly, we say it is "best calculated to getting out all the facts. . . . " That the adversary technique is useful within limits none will doubt. That it is "best" we should all doubt if we were able to be objective about the question. Despite our untested statements of self-congratulation, we know that others searching after facts—in history, geography, medicine, whatever—do not emulate our adversary system. What is much more to the point, we know that many of the rules and devices of adversary litigation as we conduct it are not geared for, but are often aptly suited to defeat, the development of the truth.
>
> We are unlikely ever to know how effectively the adversary technique would work toward truth if that were the objective of the contestants. Employed by interested parties, the process often achieves truth only as a convenience, a byproduct, or an accidental approximation. The business of the advocate, simply stated, is to win if possible without violating the law. (The phrase "if possible" is meant to modify what precedes it, but the danger of slippage is well known.) His is not the search for truth as such. To put that thought more exactly, the truth and victory are mutually incompatible for some considerable percentage of the attorneys trying cases at any given time.
>
> . . .
>
> The clearest cases are those in which the advocate has been informed directly by a competent client, or has learned from evidence too clear to admit of genuine doubt, that the client's position rests upon falsehood. It is not possible to be certain, but I believe from recollection and conversation such cases are far from rare. Much more numerous are the cases in which we manage as counsel to avoid too much knowledge. The sharp eye of the cynical lawyer becomes at strategic moments a demurely averted and filmy gaze. It may be agreeable not to

listen to the client's tape recordings of vital conversations that may contain embarrassments for the ultimate goal of vindicating the client. Unfettered by the clear prohibitions actual "knowledge" of the truth might impose, lawyers may be effective and exuberant in employing the familiar skills: techniques that make a witness look unreliable although the look stems only from counsel's artifice, cunning questions that stop short of discomfiting revelations, complaisant experts for whom some shopping may have been necessary. The credo that frees counsel for such arts is not a doctrine of truth-seeking.[6]

Monroe Freedman, a prominent academic commentator on legal ethical issues, responded to Judge Frankel's criticism that in other areas of inquiry the legal adversarial technique is not used to determine truth:

Judge Frankel directs his criticism at the adversary system itself and at the lawyer as committed adversary. Challenging the idea that the adversary system is the best method for determining the truth, Judge Frankel asserts that "we know that others searching after facts—in history, geography, medicine, whatever—do not emulate our adversary system." I would question the accuracy of that proposition, at least in the breadth in which it is stated. Moreover, I think that to the extent that other disciplines do not follow a form of adversarial process, they suffer for it. Assume, for example, a historian bent upon determining whether . . . it was militarily justifiable for the United States to devastate Nagasaki with an atomic bomb. Obviously, the historian's inquiry would not be conducted in a courtroom, but the conscientious historian's search for truth would necessarily involve a careful evaluation of evidence marshaled by other historians strongly committed to sharply differing views on those issues. In short, the process of historical research and judgment on disputed issues of history is—indeed, must be—essentially adversarial. In medicine, of course, there is typically less partisanship than in historical research because there is less room for the play of political persuasion, and less room for personal interest and bias than in the typical automobile negligence case. Nevertheless, anyone about to make an important medical decision for oneself or one's family would be well advised to get a second opinion. And if the first opinion has come from a doctor who is generally inclined to perform radical surgery, the second opinion might well be solicited from a doctor who is generally skeptical about the desirability of surgery. . . . In medical research, the situation is similar, and recent instances of dishonesty . . . illustrate the increasing importance of adversariness in medical research. . . . Now that publication of discoveries has become essential to professional advancement and to obtaining large grants of money, rigorous verification, as through replication by a skeptical colleague, has become a common requirement.[7]

Freedman's effort to analogize the trial to the pursuit of truth in other disciplines misses the mark. The scientist who checks the accuracy of the research of another is making an objective effort to determine the validity of the latter's work; he is not hired to make the best case for the validity of the research or its invalidity. And certainly he is not supposed to withhold information that would bear on its validity or invalidity.

Freedman's surgeon may well have a bias in favor of cutting. If so, it is a failing of his. He is expected to make an effort to overcome his bias. The physician offering the second opinion may also have a bias, but he too is expected to make an effort to overcome it. It is unprofessional for a physician to offer anything other than an objective judgment.

The same principles apply to the determination of truth in the social sciences. That there is often bias is indisputable, but it is always unprofessional. In the law, bias is a professional obligation. There may be an adversarial quality to the practices in other areas, as described by Freedman, but these practices purport to be an objective double-checking for accuracy. That is very different from the adversarial practice of law.

If our form of litigation is an ineffective means of determining the truth, it is not because of its adversary nature as such, but rather because of the practices and tactics that are permitted or required. Conflicting advocacy, with proper constraints, can assist in the search for truth. The problem is not the existence of an adversary system, but rather the rules that govern it.

A good deal of law practice has to do with disputes, some of which are resolved in the courts; most are resolved by negotiated settlement either before or after suit is brought. Zealous advocacy is employed in the negotiated settlement, but there is no impartial party to determine the facts and the legal result. The parties make their determination based on the perceived chances of success in court and the costs of a trial. The lawyer's posture and objectives are essentially the same as in a trial, although the setting is different.

On the other hand, a good deal of law practice is concerned with the transfer of property, the preparation of contracts, the organization of business enterprises, and the like. Although these transactions usually involve parties having different or conflicting interests, frequently the parties are friendly and cooperative and the role of the lawyer is nonadversarial. Sometimes, however, the transaction involves contentious arm's-length bargaining in which zealous advocacy is called for. The lawyer strives to obtain as much as he can for his client by the use of his client's economic power or strategic advantage. Justice—that is, fairness—does not have much of a role, if any.

The peculiar partisanship of lawyers, inside and outside the courtroom, is the characteristic that distinguishes the practice of law from other professions. Richard Wasserstrom, a professor of philosophy and a lawyer, has commented on this:

> ... The lawyer—and especially the lawyer as advocate—directly says and affirms things. The lawyer makes the case for the client. He or she tries to ex-

plain, persuade and convince others that the client's cause should prevail. The lawyer lives with and within a dilemma that is not shared by other professionals. If the lawyer actually believes everything that he or she asserts on behalf of the client, then it appears to be proper to regard the lawyer as in fact embracing and endorsing the points of view that he or she articulates. If the lawyer does not in fact believe what is urged by way of argument, if the lawyer is only playing a role, then it appears to be proper to tax the lawyer with hypocrisy and insincerity. To be sure, actors in a play take on roles and say things that the characters, not the actors, believe. But we know it is a play and that they are actors. The law courts are not, however, theaters, and the lawyers both talk about justice and they genuinely seek to persuade. The fact that the lawyer's words, thoughts, and convictions are, apparently, for sale and at the service of the client helps us, I think, to understand the peculiar hostility which is more than occasionally uniquely directed by lay persons toward lawyers. The verbal, role-differentiated behavior of the lawyer *qua* advocate puts the lawyer's integrity into question in a way that distinguishes the lawyer from the other professionals.[8]

CONFIDENTIALITY

A cardinal principle of the practice of law is the duty of confidentiality owed by the lawyer to the client. It is a most significant means to the achievement of the client's objective. The professional rules provide, "A lawyer shall not reveal information relating to representation of a client unless the client consents after consultation, except for disclosures that are impliedly authorized in order to carry out the representation."[9] The last clause has to do with disclosures that the lawyer makes in order to further the objectives of her representation. To represent the client adequately the lawyer must obtain all relevant information from the client and others. In order to do this effectively, there must be the assurance of confidentiality. Some information that the lawyer needs may be personal or may be damaging to the client if disclosed to third parties. The client, or others on his behalf, may be reluctant to disclose fully unless they are assured that the revelation of such information will not go beyond the lawyer. Confidentiality is important in the nonlitigation context as well as in the context of civil or criminal litigation.

There are, however, several exceptions to the duty of confidentiality that are not in the interest of the client. In most states the lawyer may disclose confidences concerning "The intention of his client to commit a crime and the information necessary to prevent the crime."[10] Note that the lawyer *may* (not must) make such disclosures.

In addition, the lawyer *may* reveal information reasonably necessary "to establish a claim or defense on behalf of the lawyer in a controversy between the lawyer and the client, to establish a defense to a criminal charge or civil claim against the lawyer based upon conduct in which the client was involved, or to respond to allegations in any proceeding concerning the lawyer's representation of the client."[11]

There are further qualifications to the duty of confidentiality. If the lawyer has presented evidence and later learns that it is false, she *must* inform the court of the falsity, even if this results in the disclosure of confidential information.[12] If the lawyer representing a criminal defendant knows that her client intends to testify falsely, and she cannot dissuade him, she *must* inform the court of this matter even if this results in the disclosure of confidential information.[13]

The purpose of confidentiality is to facilitate the lawyer's efforts to obtain what the client is entitled to under the law. If the client is seeking the lawyer's assistance in connection with the prospective commission of a crime, confidentiality with respect to the matter obviously has nothing to do with what the client is entitled to under the law. It follows that the lawyer should not be bound to keep that information confidential, as the professional rules provide. Since someone may be harmed by the crime and there is no justificatory purpose served by confidentiality, it also follows that the lawyer may have a moral duty to act to prevent the crime from occurring, but the professional rules impose no such obligation.

The legal profession has seen to it that the duty of confidentiality has no application where the interests of the lawyer are concerned. If the lawyer sues the client for her fee, is sued for malpractice by the client, is charged with ethical misconduct by the profession in connection with the representation, or is charged criminally or civilly in connection with conduct in which the client is involved, the duty of confidentiality does not apply. As we have seen in several examples in Chapter 1, confidentiality is required at the expense of extraordinary harm to third persons, but the legal profession has seen to it that the lawyer is treated differently. This is professional special-interest legislation in its rawest form.

A criminal defendant has the right to testify in his own defense, but if the lawyer knows that he intends to testify falsely, she must inform the court, despite the fact that her knowledge is derived from confidential information. If the lawyer has presented evidence in a civil or criminal case believing it to be true and subsequently learns of its falsity, she must inform the court, despite the fact that this knowledge is derived from confidential information. This is consistent with the rationale of confidentiality; perjurious testimony obviously does not contribute to the purpose of providing to the client what the law allows.

On the other hand, suppose the lawyer in a civil case knows of evidence that would be destructive to her client's case, and the attorney for the opposing party has failed to discover that evidence. There has been no deliberate concealment of the evidence by the lawyer. As a result of this circumstance, her client obtains a court judgment to which he was not entitled under the law. The duty of exclusive and zealous dedication to the client's interest, of which confidentiality is a part, thus produces a miscarriage of justice in this instance. The opposing party has been harmed; there is no consideration that outweighs this harm in the moral scales. The lawyer is forbidden to present false evidence in court because that perverts the purpose of the trial—the pursuit of truth. But the withholding of the truth from the courtroom has the same effect, yet is mandatory. This turns justice into a game, and an immoral one at that.

There is an interesting interplay in the relationship between confidentiality and the duty not to present false evidence. Confidentiality serves the purpose of encouraging the client to tell all to the lawyer so that the lawyer may represent him adequately. If the client gives the lawyer information damaging to his case, the lawyer cannot present testimony favorable to her client that conflicts with it. The effect of the client's disclosure is to limit the lawyer's presentation of her case to what the client is entitled to under the law. This is as it should be. The client is entitled to confidentiality, but he is only entitled to what the law allows. There is, of course, a cynical approach to this situation; the client may be better off if he does not tell all to the lawyer. Some lawyers are careful not to probe too deeply for fear that they will learn something that will impede the effectiveness of their presentation of their case.

Examples of Confidentiality

Let us now explore the duty of confidentiality by reviewing several examples from Chapter 1. In Example 15 (Confidentiality: Life-Threatening Injury) the lawyer represents a client who negligently injured the pedestrian-plaintiff while driving his automobile. The lawyer hires a physician to examine the pedestrian and learns that the pedestrian suffered an aortic aneurysm which is life-threatening. The pedestrian is apparently unaware of his condition; his physician presumably did not detect it in his examination. The lawyer for the driver does not disclose the injury until after a settlement agreement is formally entered into, the amount of which does not reflect the seriousness of the pedestrian's injury. The settlement is valid. The pedestrian has received less than what the law entitles him to; the negligent party pays less than what the law calls for.

Clearly, in this example exclusive dedication to the client's interest and confidentiality have not served the purpose of providing what the law allows; rather they have disserved it. The pedestrian has been harmed financially, and there is no consideration that justifies this harm in the moral scales. Nor is there any moral justification for the risk of death that is the consequence of the silence. The lawyer cannot present perjurious testimony, but she must withhold vital evidence that deprives the opposing party of his due. This makes no moral sense.

The purpose of confidentiality is to facilitate the achievement of what the client is entitled to under the law. To represent the client adequately to achieve what the law allows him, the lawyer should learn as much as she can. This may include information that is damaging to the client. Under the professional rules the lawyer is not permitted to present evidence that contradicts the damaging information; that is to say, the lawyer cannot present evidence that she knows to be false. Learning the bad news prevents the lawyer from making the "best possible case" on behalf of her client. In effect, the client is penalized by telling all to the lawyer. It has been maintained that this proscription is inconsistent with the purposes of confidentiality, and that the lawyer should be permitted to present evidence favorable to her case that she knows, from confidential information, is false,[14] but that position has never been accepted by the profession. Confidentiality does not justify the use of perjury to achieve what the client is not entitled to. Similarly, there is no justification for silence that enables the client to obtain what he is not entitled to. Perjury and silence inflict harm upon the adversary without adequate justification.

It may be argued that the justification for remaining silent about damaging information received from the client is the implicit promise of confidentiality made by the lawyer to the client. That is to say, there is more to the duty of confidentiality than the achievement of what the law allows the client; confidentiality is a personal commitment. We have seen, however, that under the existing rules, confidentiality is waived for information regarding the intention to commit a crime, for information establishing that false testimony has been presented, for information establishing that a criminal defendant intends to testify perjuriously, and for information that serves certain interests of the lawyer. Confidentiality is a qualified professional commitment defined by the rules, with exceptions, of which some further justice. There is no personal commitment that extends beyond the professional rules. The position taken here is that the rules should further qualify confidentiality to make it clear that it does not apply to any information that, if withheld, would provide the client with more than the law allows.

In Example 16 (Confidentiality: Past Fraud), the lawyer learned that her client, Computer, Inc., had defrauded banks in transactions in which the lawyer had represented the firm without knowing about the fraud. The lawyer terminated the representation when she learned of the fraud. The company retained another lawyer and continued its fraudulent practices with the assistance of the innocent second lawyer. The first lawyer never told the second lawyer, the banks, or anyone else of the fraud. Ultimately the fraudulent practices became known. The professional rules forbade the

first lawyer from disclosing the prior fraud of the client and from disclosing
the potential for future fraud because she did not know that the fraud
would continue. (It is assumed here that the prospective fraud would be
criminal; the lawyer would be forbidden to disclose the client's intention to
commit any *non*criminal wrong in the future even if she was certain it
would occur.)

Confidentiality with respect to the past fraud, in which the lawyer unwittingly participated, is not justified because it does not serve the purpose of
achieving what the law allows the client. If the lawyer had discovered the
past fraud while it was taking place, she would have been forbidden to assist the client and would have had to terminate the representation under the
professional rules.[15] If the lawyer was convinced that the client would con-
summate the fraud after her withdrawal, she would be permitted to disclose the prospective fraud (assuming it was criminal) under the professional rules.

What has been learned in confidence prevents the lawyer from continuing to serve the client to achieve what the law does not allow and permits
the lawyer to disclose in order to prevent the client from achieving his criminal objective. If those are the consequences under the rules if the fraud is
known by the lawyer contemporaneously, then confidentiality is not justified when the lawyer learns of the fraud after the fact. Imposing the rule of
confidentiality upon the lawyer after the wrong is discovered has the effect
of aiding the client in keeping his illegal benefit and impeding redress for
the defrauded party. In this circumstance confidentiality contributes to
harm without adequate justification.

In Example 18 (Confidentiality: Unprosecuted Homicide) the lawyer represented a person who was being prosecuted for homicide. During the
course of the representation the client told the lawyer that some years ago
he had murdered a man—an act for which he was never prosecuted–and
that another person had been convicted of the crime and was serving a life
sentence. The lawyer was forbidden to reveal this information under the
professional rules.

This information is unrelated to what the client is or is not entitled to in
this case. Silence does not affect the justice of the result in this case. The responsible lawyer seeks to learn as much as possible that may be related directly or indirectly to the case, in order to prepare her presentation, avoid
surprise at trial, assess the client's vulnerability to cross-examination, and
assess settlement opportunities. This probing may result in the disclosure of
past illegal conduct that has not been corrected or revealed.

It is plausible to maintain that confidentiality of such damaging information serves the goal of providing the client with what the law allows. This is
because the information is obtained from the thorough investigation that is
necessary for the proper preparation of the client's case, and the confiden-

tiality of such information does not provide the client with an illegal benefit as far as the immediate representation is concerned.

Certainly such confidentiality has the effect of protecting the client with respect to his past illegal conduct. Nevertheless, the value of confidentiality in this circumstance may outweigh in the moral scales the value of the disclosure of the unrelated past wrong. Confidentiality to some degree is essential for thorough representation. If the client risks the revelation of unrelated past wrongs that he communicates to his lawyer, the impact upon the representation would be devastating.

It is one thing to set confidentiality aside in the interest of justice in the immediate matter; it is another to set it aside with respect to all past wrongs not directly related to the resolution of the specific subject of the representation. Moral judgment involves the drawing of lines; this seems to be a sensible place for it. If the system accepts that lawyers are to serve as agents and fiduciaries for clients, confidentiality must have a place in the relationship. If it is not applicable to this circumstance, it has little significance. The lawyer's representation should not be used as a means of achieving what the law does not allow; in the case of confidentiality with respect to past unrelated illegal conduct, this has not occurred.

Suppose in this example the client tells his lawyer that he committed the homicide for which he is being prosecuted. Based on the preceding discussion concerning the representation of a defendant in a civil matter, it seems that there should be no confidentiality because it would assist the client to avoid the legal consequences of his criminal act. In the context of criminal representation, however, confidentiality may be justified. For one thing, the Constitutional privilege against self-incrimination gives the criminal defendant the right to refuse to testify at his trial. The value of human dignity takes precedence over the search for truth. If the lawyer could reveal the client's confession to her, the client's Constitutional privilege would be undermined. The civil plaintiff and defendant, on the other hand, can be compelled to testify by the opposing party. There are other reasons for having different confidentiality rules in the context of criminal representation, as will be discussed later in this chapter.

In Example 17 (Confidentiality: Child Abuse) the lawyer represented a divorced mother, who had custody of her two very young children, in connection with financial matters such as social service benefits and child support payments from the father that were in default. In the course of the representation the lawyer discovers that her client is unstable and sometimes beats her children. There is a law that requires disclosure to public authorities by those who know of such abuse, but the law does not state whether the lawyer's duty of confidentiality supersedes the statutory duty. The professional rules provide that the lawyer's duty of confidentiality should supersede the statute. Such information would probably justify taking custody of the children from the client, but the information is not known by others and her custody is not being challenged. So long as she has custody she is entitled to child support and other welfare benefits. The fact of abuse is not directly at issue with respect to the matters in which the lawyer is representing the client.

Does the lawyer, by maintaining confidentiality, assist the client in this representation to obtain what the law does not allow the client? Is this analogous to the withholding of knowledge of the aortic aneurysm or to the withholding of knowledge of the past unrelated homicide? Because disclosure could result in loss of custody and, as a consequence, loss of the social service benefits and child support that are the subject of the representation, this case seems to be more analogous to the aortic aneurysm case. Confidentiality therefore is not justified.

The thrust of our discussion is that there is inadequate justification for confidentiality with respect to information that assists the client in obtaining what the law does not allow. In the absence of a duty of confidentiality, the lawyer may nevertheless choose to remain silent, in which case the client is assisted in the same antisocial way. It is immoral for a person to stand by and allow something to happen that harms someone else when that person could prevent the harm without excessive cost to himself. If professional rules of behavior were to require that the lawyer disclose information harmful to her client and helpful to another, there should be no cost to the individual lawyer. Lawyers would become in this context instruments of justice.

It will, of course, be argued that if lawyers are permitted or required to disclose damaging information, it will induce clients to withhold such information from the lawyer. There is, however, an incentive for the client to be less than candid with his lawyer under the existing rules. The lawyer is forbidden to present evidence that she knows is false; if the lawyer does not know of certain damaging information, she may be able innocently to present false evidence that is helpful to her client.

The denial of confidentiality may be one more incentive for the client to be less than honest with his lawyer, but the reason for a rule denying confidentiality is the same as the reason for the existing rule that the lawyer cannot present evidence she knows to be false. If the client chooses to be less than candid with his lawyer, he does so at his risk, such as surprise at trial, the expense of a futile trial if the gamble does not pay off, and the possibility of prosecution for perjury. In any event, the lawyer should not be allowed to be an accomplice to injustice by action or silence.

Active Harm and Passive Harm

On the one hand, the lawyer is prohibited from presenting evidence helpful to his client that he knows is perjurious from confidential information received from his client. On the other hand, the lawyer is required to maintain confidentiality concerning information received from his client that is helpful to the adversary but unknown to him. The purpose of confidentiality is to encourage the client to level with his lawyer. In the first situation the client's revelation limits what the lawyer can do for him and serves the end of justice. In the second situation the lawyer's silence harms the client's adversary and disserves the end of justice. In the first situation if the lawyer were to present the perjurious testimony he would be deceiving the judge and the jury. In the second situation the lawyer's silence has the same effect. Why does the law condemn the active harm (deception) and condone the passive harm (nondisclosure)?

There is an analogy in the law. If I hold an infant's head underwater until she drowns, I'm guilty of homicide. If, however, I observe someone else's infant, for whom I have not undertaken any responsibility, struggling to survive in three feet of water, and although I am able to save her without risk to myself, I choose to do nothing, I have committed no crime, and I am not civilly liable.[16] Maybe the homicidal conduct is a greater moral wrong than the failure to rescue, but if so there isn't much difference. The law does not impose positive behavioral duties to do good where no responsibility has been undertaken. The law does not require one to be a Good Samaritan. The moral duty of beneficence, which requires one to do good unless it involves excessive cost or risk to oneself, is not incorporated into the law.

Why is this? Probably the principal reason has to do with line-drawing. The situation described is easy. But suppose it is five feet of water and the potential rescuer cannot swim and is terrified of the water. Suppose there is an auto accident, a person in one of the cars is unconscious, and the motor is running; a passerby observes the situation but does not act because he is fearful of an explosion. Suppose one observes smoke coming from the next-door neighbor's house where a family with two infant children lives. Calling 911 is easy, but should one be required to enter a house that may be in flames? There are myriad problematic situations.

In the law a duty not to harm in a specific manner, such as assault or theft, can be expressed clearly and be effectively enforced. The same may not be true with respect to doing good in a specific manner. Compelling a person to make a problematic judgment of rescue or face possible criminal sanction or civil liability may be asking too much of human nature. It is significant that one can avoid inflicting harm, but one cannot avoid being placed in a position of rescue.[17]

The lawyer's silence that impedes justice is a form of passive harm similar to the failure to rescue. However, to require the lawyer to disclose in order to effect justice is different in a significant respect from imposing a duty to rescue. Such disclosure relates to matters that can be defined and enforced with as much precision as is characteristic of legal rules: The lawyer must disclose information that is helpful to the adversary's claim or defense. Such a requirement gives justice priority over the interests of the client, but, as described above, loyalty to the interests of the client is substantially qualified under the rules relating to confidentiality as they presently exist.

There is another analogy in the law concerning active harm and passive harm. Assume that two parties enter into a contract of some kind or a sale of property. One of the parties deliberately misrepresents a fact that has a material bearing on the transaction, and the misrepresentation induces the other party to enter into the transaction. The deceived party may recover any damages he may have suffered or rescind the transaction. This conduct constitutes fraud.

Now a passive form of the same harm. One party to a contract or a sale of property is aware of a material fact bearing on the transaction that is unfavorable to the interests of the other party. The first party knows that the other party is ignorant of this unfavorable material fact. He remains silent, and the transaction is consummated. Soon thereafter the other party discovers the unfavorable fact. The traditional legal conclusion is that the transaction is valid; the informed party has no obligation to tell the uninformed party the unfavorable fact.[18] This reflects the individualistic nature of our system of law; each person has to look out for himself. The rationale is that society is better off if each person understands that he has the responsibility to protect his own interests.

In recent years there has been some movement in the law on this issue. Courts in some states have decided that in some types of transactions such silence is the functional equivalent of active misrepresentation. The silent party may be liable for damages suffered by the other party or the transaction may be rescinded.[19] The traditional individualistic legal conclusion, however, remains the prevailing rule, the liability for nondisclosure being the exception.

The occasional judicial decision that silence is the functional equivalent of fraud supports the position that the lawyer's silence regarding facts favorable to the adversary is the functional equivalent of presenting testimony that is known to be perjurious. In some instances the adversary's lawyer may be delinquent in his efforts to discover the information on his own. The individualistic position is that each party should be responsible for protecting his own interests. But in the case of the delinquent lawyer, it is the lawyer's client who suffers if there is no disclosure.

There is a provision in the professional rules that provides some support for the position that the lawyer's silence is unjustified. The rules provide that if the lawyer presents testimony he does not know is false and later in the trial discovers that the testimony was false, the lawyer is required to disclose its falsity to the court.[20] Silence in this circumstance would be a form of passive harm functionally equivalent to the knowing presentation of perjurious testimony.

Confidentiality in Criminal Representation

We have been considering the moral requirement of the disclosure of information damaging to the client primarily in the civil context. The same conclusion may not be appropriate in the representation of a person being prosecuted for a crime. As was mentioned above, the confession of guilt by the criminal defendant to his lawyer must be confidential. The criminal defendant has the Constitutional privilege to refuse to testify; human dignity takes precedence over the pursuit of truth. If the criminal defendant's confession to his lawyer could be revealed, the Constitutional privilege would be subverted. The civil defendant in litigation, on the other hand, can be compelled to testify by the opposing party.

The lawyer may receive information damaging to the criminal client's defense other than from the client. There is no Constitutional privilege relative to such information. For purposes of the justification for confidentiality, should this information be treated differently from similar information in the civil context? On the surface, it seems not. The withholding of the information assists the client in avoiding the consequences of his criminal conduct. But because of the stigma of criminal conviction and the possible sanction of imprisonment, the legal system has established special protections for the criminally accused. Should the stigma and the prospect of imprisonment produce a different moral result with respect to confidentiality?

As we have mentioned, the criminal defendant has the Constitutional right not to testify at his own trial. The burden of proof imposed upon the state in its prosecution of the criminal defendant is much greater than the burden of proof imposed upon the civil plaintiff in its suit against the civil defendant. The state must prove the criminal defendant's guilt beyond a reasonable doubt. The civil plaintiff must prove the defendant's liability by a preponderance of the evidence; that is to say, the plaintiff must establish that it is more likely than not that the defendant did what the plaintiff charges him with. It is understood that the criminal standard often results in the acquittal of the guilty. The criminal prosecutor is also Constitutionally required to turn over to the defendant evidence that tends to exculpate the defendant. There is no such Constitutional duty imposed on the civil plaintiff. The extraordinary protections afforded the criminal defendant are the consequence of the moral position that it is better that guilty people be acquitted than that an innocent person be convicted. A criminal conviction can destroy a person's life.

It should be emphasized that the lawyer who has information damaging to her criminal defendant client cannot present contradictory evidence she knows to be false. If the purpose of trial is the search for truth, why should the professional duty of silence be morally acceptable in the criminal trial? The pursuit of truth is impeded as much by silence as it is by the presentation of false evidence. On the other side of the ledger, the legal system, for other moral reasons, is very protective of the criminal defendant.

It has been said that conventional moral judgment should not be applied to circumstances in which moral strictures conflict with an elemental human response. For example, a parent should not be morally criticized for lying to save his guilty child from criminal prosecution. The same principle probably applies here. Where a person's freedom is at stake, any violation of confidence concerning incriminating information by the lawyer would be felt to be a devastating betrayal. Maybe that weighs in the moral scales as well.

The defense of a person charged with crime is unique in the practice of law. All things considered, confidentiality as presently practiced is justified in this form of representation.

TACTICS

Now we examine the justification for several specific tactics used by lawyers in litigation. It is reiterated that tactics that deceive or harm others or impede justice can only be morally justified on the basis that they serve the purpose of achieving for the client what the law allows or some other social or moral end that outweighs the prima facie immoral conduct. In Example 1 (Discrediting the Truthful Witness) the lawyer represented a criminal defendant charged with robbery. The client admits to his lawyer that he committed the crime. He does not testify at his trial. The lawyer attempts to impeach the credibility of a truthful prosecution witness who observed the crime by establishing on cross-examination that she had been drinking heavily prior to the crime, that she had a violent argument with the defendant shortly before the crime, and that she had convictions for shoplifting. The lawyer's efforts are designed to mislead the jury and inflict harm upon the truthful witness. This professionally permissible conduct is immoral unless it can be justified by some good that outweighs it on the moral scales. The only purpose of the deception and harm is to obtain an undeserved acquittal for the client, hardly a social good.

It may be argued that in order for the lawyer to obtain for her client all that the law allows, she must obtain all the information—the helpful and the damaging—from the client; if the damaging information prevents the lawyer from attempting to discredit a truthful witness, the client is deterred from providing his lawyer with complete information. But the lawyer is forbidden to present testimony helpful to her client that she knows is perjurious because of information provided by the client. There is no moral distinction between presenting perjury and discrediting the truthful witness; both are efforts to obscure the truth and frustrate justice. Indeed, discrediting the witness is morally worse because it also inflicts harm upon the innocent witness.

In Example 2 (Exploiting the Adversary's Mistake) the lawyer represented a criminal defendant who admitted to his lawyer that he committed the robbery for which he was being prosecuted. Because of the theft of his watch and his injury, the victim mistakenly identified the hour the crime occurred as ten o'clock rather than nine o'clock when the crime in fact occurred. The lawyer presented truthful testimony of two friends of the defendant that he was at a bar with them at ten o'clock. Under the professional rules it is permissible for the lawyer to present such testimony that has the effect of misleading the jury.

A tactic that misleads requires justification. None exists here. The objective is an undeserved acquittal. If it were impermissible to present this testimony, the lawyer would be denied the opportunity to make an alibi for her client because she had properly obtained complete information (admission of guilt) from her client. The present rules "penalize" the lawyer and her client by denying the lawyer the opportunity to present perjurious testimony in conflict with what she knows to be true. The lawyer cannot subvert justice by the use of perjury. But the truthful testimony of the client's friends serves the same function as perjury. The present rules see the harm of perjury as outweighing the good of thorough investigation; the same result should follow with respect to truthful testimony that has the purpose and effect of obscuring the truth.

If the criminal defense lawyer representing a client she knows to be guilty is not permitted to attempt to discredit a truthful prosecution witness or to present truthful testimony that provides an alibi for the client because of the mistake of the victim or the prosecutor, what is left for the lawyer to do on behalf of her client? There is a great deal that can be done. The law requires that the prosecution prove its case beyond a reasonable doubt. That is very different from the civil standard that the plaintiff prove his case by a preponderance of the evidence, *i.e.*, that it is more likely than not that the plaintiff's account is correct. The lawyer for the criminal defendant can argue that the evidence presented by the prosecution does not meet the required standard for conviction based on gaps or uncertainty that may exist in the prosecution's case. The issue before the jury is not whether they believe the defendant committed the crime, but whether they believe it has been proved beyond a reasonable doubt. Thus the lawyer is able to provide the client what the law allows him.

In addition, the lawyer may concede that her client committed the act, but may present truthful evidence or argue that certain elements relating to the client's intent or the degree of harm to the victim were not sufficiently established to warrant conviction for the specific crime for which the client is being prosecuted. If successful this defense may result in a conviction of a lesser crime or in an acquittal, depending on circumstances.

The lawyer may concede that her client committed the act but present truthful evidence that her client is not guilty of the crime because of some form of insanity or other reason that excused the act.[21]

In Example 3 (Better Not to Probe) the lawyer represented a wife in divorce and child custody litigation. The client and her close friends told the lawyer of the husband's shocking neglect and psychological abuse of the children, aged three and four. The lawyer lived in the same neighborhood as his client and knew the husband slightly. The lawyer is skeptical of what he has been told about the husband but he does not investigate further. The lawyer presented the testimony. This practice is commonplace and is generally accepted as professionally permissible.

Clearly the tactic of not probing does not serve the purpose of assisting the lawyer in obtaining for his client what the law allows. To the extent that the failure to probe results in the presentation of testimony that is false, it is an indirect form of deception. There is no consequential moral or social good to justify it.

Now, assume that probing would establish that the information initially obtained, which is favorable to the client, is untrue. If the lawyer does not probe, his client may be better off than if he did. The principle of zealous advocacy appears to support the lawyer's acceptance of the information initially obtained. This circumstance simply and vividly illustrates the issue of what the lawyer's function is and what it should be. Is it the lawyer's role to achieve for his client whatever he can without violating the law or professional rules? Most lawyers would respond in the affirmative. Should the lawyer's role be to achieve for his client whatever his client is entitled to under the law? The latter is a very different proposition from the former.

Let us return for a moment to the proposition that supports the lawyer's participation in the legal but antisocial or immoral objective of the client, as discussed in Chapter 2. In the simplest terms, the lawyer is morally justified in assisting the client in obtaining what the law allows in a fundamentally just legal system. Is it not contradictory for the lawyer to use tactics that may be in conflict with this principle, that is, to obtain for his client what he is *not* entitled to under the law?

In Example 4 (Stating the Law Before Asking for the Facts) the lawyer provides the client with a general statement of the law applicable to his problem before he asks the client for the relevant facts. The client then is in a position to assess the consequences of the information he relates to the lawyer; this may tempt the client to tailor the "facts" in a manner favorable to his legal position. This consideration militates against the propriety of what the lawyer has done.

However, memory is often indistinct and elusive, and articulation is often imprecise and disordered. People sometimes blurt out things that are not accurate. If subsequent adjustments are made by the client, the conscientious lawyer has an ethical problem of how to deal with the contradictions. Legal consequences tend to focus the mind; greater clarity of recall and articulation may be effected by providing the client with a legal frame of reference. There is the additional factor of fairness to the client; he is entitled to know the consequences of what he reports to his lawyer.

Certainly the practice of telling the client the law before getting the facts may be misused by the client. Nonetheless, the interests of accuracy of recall and articulation and of fairness to the client probably justify the practice. Some lawyers, however, consider that the risk of abuse outweighs the other considerations; that is certainly a reasonable position. The practice is permissible under the rules, and, on balance, that seems proper.

In Example 5 (Dilatory Tactics) the lawyer represents a drug manufacturer who sells a drug that a federal agency in all likelihood is going to ban from the market in the near future because of certain undesirable side effects. There are several responsible scientists who doubt that the tests on the drug's side effects were valid. The view of the scientific community, however, is overwhelmingly to the contrary. The several scientists have not had an opportunity to present their position to the agency. The lawyer and the client know that the chance that their testimony will alter the agency's conclusion is minuscule. However, if the lawyer petitions for a hearing to present their testimony, the ban on the drug may be delayed for several months. The client has a large inventory of the drug that could be sold during this time. At the client's direction, the lawyer petitions for the hearing. This action would not have been taken but for the delay that it would cause.

The lawyer's conduct is permissible under the professional rules. Action that has no merit (that is frivolous) and causes delay is impermissible, but the petition is not frivolous. The testimony of the scientists is serious. The lawyer's motive, however, is not to achieve for his client what the law allows but to avoid, at least for a period of time, the proper application of the law to his client. The harm caused is that the government is put to an expense, and health risks for consumers are extended.

On the one hand, if the action would not be taken but for the delay, it should not be professionally permissible to take the action. If, on the other hand, the chance of success is minuscule, but the client wants to exhaust all the possibilities of avoiding the ban, the action should be professionally permissible even though delay results. Often it is not clear on which side of the line a tactic falls, but lawyers are accustomed to dealing with problems in the "gray area."

In Example 6 (Describing the Consequences of Criminal Conduct) a lawyer represents a chemical manufacturer seeking assistance with new environmental regulations that deal with its chemical effluent. Violation could result in a criminal prosecution. The client inquires as to the realities of governmental enforcement. The lawyer responds that in the event a violation is detected, the violator is likely to be given a period of time to come into compliance if the violation does not exceed by more than 30 percent that which is allowed by law. In addition, if the violation does not exceed the legal maximum by more than 15 percent, the government does not attempt to impose sanctions, due to understaffing. The lawyer's response is professionally permissible. He cannot counsel a client to engage, or assist a client, in criminal conduct, but he can inform the client of the legal consequences of any proposed course of conduct.[22] The lawyer has done the latter.

When the client asks the lawyer what the chance of prosecution is, and the lawyer replies that it is very unlikely, the reply may have the effect of encouraging the client to engage in the criminal conduct. It is very close to counseling the client to engage in criminal conduct. Indeed, if the lawyer volunteers such information without being asked, such conduct may well constitute counseling the client to engage in criminal conduct. To deny the client the facts of criminal enforcement when he asks, however, is to limit information concerning the operation of our government. The availability of such information is a social good that outweighs the possibility that the information may be used by the client to do what the law forbids.

What is missing in the rules is a requirement that the lawyer remind the client of his duty as a citizen to comply with the law. It is remarkable that there is no such explicit provision in the rule concerned with the permissibility of informing the client of the consequences of a proposed course of conduct that is criminal or fraudulent.

Example 8 (Lying in Negotiations) is concerned with willful misstatements of fact by a lawyer in negotiations for the settlement of a dispute. The rules provide that a lawyer "shall not knowingly . . . make a false statement of material fact or law to a third person."[23] An explanatory section of the rules states, "Under generally accepted conventions in negotiation, certain types of statements ordinarily are not taken as statements of material fact. Estimates of price or value placed on the subject of a transaction and a party's intentions as to an acceptable settlement of a claim are in this category."[24]

The rules, in effect, authorize the lawyer to lie in order to assist the client in an out-of-court resolution of a legal dispute. Lying is hardly a tactic designed to achieve an approximation of what the law allows, which should be the function of settlement negotiations.[25]

Note that the rule constrains the lawyer to be truthful with respect to "material facts." Lying is permissible with respect to nonmaterial facts. The explanatory section seems to suggest that certain statements in negotiations are not treated as material facts, because it is understood that negotiators lie about such matters. The point of all this seems to be that the lie does no harm because the person to whom it is directed doesn't take the statement seriously. This is known in the commercial world as puffing and bluffing. The alleged harmless nature of this practice, however, does not stand up to analysis.

If it is true that the speaker knows that the listener knows that the speaker really doesn't mean what he's saying, then the speaker's statements will not serve the speaker's end. If the puff or the bluff is understood to be absolutely false, then it would not influence the behavior of the listener. If the speaker knew this to be the case, there would be no point in his making the statement. Although the listener may discount what the speaker is saying, if the speaker's words are to have any effect, the listener must read into them some risk that the speaker means what he says or means what he says to some extent. The speaker necessarily intends this to be the case. If the speaker is saying something that is not true, but the listener thinks that there is a 20 percent chance that it is true, or some chance that there is a degree of truth in what is said, to that extent the speaker has deceived and the conduct is a lie and is immoral.

Such conduct by lawyers has no place in a process whose purpose is to achieve some approximation of what the law provides. It is also unworthy of someone who purports to be a member of a profession. Clients may, if they are so inclined, engage in such practices on a regular basis. When they hire lawyers to represent them, they should expect that the standard of behavior is different. Lying in negotiations is morally wrong; there is no consideration that justifies its use.

In Example 9 (Custody Blackmail) a lawyer represents a husband in his negotiations with his wife concerning a divorce. The wife wants custody of the children; the husband does not want custody. The lawyer advises his client that a custody demand by him could be a bargaining device to reduce his wife's claim for alimony and child support, because of her fear of losing in court on custody. The husband agrees to making the demand for custody. It is understood that if the wife should call her husband's bluff by not yielding on her demands and by challenging the husband's custody claim in court, he would withdraw his claim. This ploy, sometimes referred to as "custody blackmail," is often used by divorce lawyers. It is assumed to be professionally permissible.

The husband is misrepresenting his intention. He says that he will press his claim for custody, but he has no intention of doing so. The misrepresentation of one's intention in order to induce certain conduct by another is a form of fraud. The lawyer is forbidden to counsel the client to engage in fraud or to assist the client in fraudulent conduct.[26] This misrepresentation, however, is made in the context of negotiations. We have seen that the rules explicitly allow lawyers to misrepresent certain matters in negotiations, such as the "value placed on the subject of a transaction." It is far from clear that this comes within those terms. The rules mention that situation, however, only as an example; the generality is that misrepresentations that have become conventions in negotiations are permissible. Perhaps "custody blackmail" has become such a convention.

Misrepresentation has no place in a process whose purpose should be to achieve some approximation of what the law provides. Psychological pressure, persuasion, and disparate economic impacts of litigation can all contribute to the terms of a settlement in a way that is not wholly consonant with what the law provides. Settlement is an imperfect process. But the lawyer's misrepresentation, or her assistance to the misrepresenting client, distorts the object of the process excessively. There is no consideration that justifies this immoral behavior.

In Example 10 (Using a False Identity), the lawyer represented a client who was sued for negligently injuring the plaintiff. An aspect of the plaintiff's claim for damages was that the injury prevented him from performing certain business functions. The lawyer was skeptical of this and hired a private investigator to look into it. The lawyer knew that the private investigator used false identities when necessary, and he did so in this case. He discovered that the claim for business damages was false.

Lawyers are forbidden to participate in fraudulent, deceitful, or dishonest conduct, and the use of the false identity is literally within this prohibition.[27] It is not clear, however, that this form of dishonesty is intended to be covered by the prohibition. It certainly is common practice for criminal prosecutors to use informants who disguise their identity, and sometimes lawyers in noncriminal matters use similar tactics. In view of its long-standing use, the practice may be professionally permissible.[28]

A tactic that deceives is immoral unless it serves a purpose that outweighs it in the moral scales. Here the purpose of the deceit is to determine the truth and achieve for the client what the law allows. The practice of deceit usually serves the purpose of impeding justice, but not in this example. Maybe this is sufficient justification. However, dishonesty and deceit, even when employed in a worthy cause, may contribute to public cynicism and disrespect for our societal institutions. Certainly deceit should be employed sparingly. It is suggested that if the use of a subterfuge is essential to the detection of crime, the rules should permit it in that circumstance, but otherwise it should be forbidden.

In Example 11 (Inserting an Illegal Clause), a lawyer for a landlord who owns a number of apartment buildings includes in every lease a provision that the landlord has no obligation to make any repairs. This provision is in conflict with a state statute that requires landlords to make repairs, an obligation that cannot be modified by the terms of a lease. The landlord and his lawyer are aware of the statute. Tenants never consult a lawyer before signing the lease and are usually unaware of their statutory rights.

The purpose of the provision is to discourage tenants from asking for or insisting upon repairs. The tenants have been misled to believe that the lease denies them any legal claim for repairs. This is a form of deception. The lawyer is forbidden to assist his client in criminal or fraudulent conduct; clearly no crime is involved. The lawyer is also forbidden to engage in fraudulent, dishonest, or deceitful conduct. The tenant in this example can discover his rights by consulting an attorney, but in practical application, he is not likely to do so. Lawyers often overreach in this way in the preparation of contracts when their bargaining position permits it. It is not clear whether this relatively mild form of deception is covered by the prohibition upon fraudulent, dishonest, and deceitful conduct. Its frequent use, as well as the absence of any specific prohibition in the rules, suggests that it is professionally permissible.

Deception is morally wrong unless there is a compelling social or moral consideration that justifies it. No such justification exists here. The purpose of this deception is to achieve for the client what the law does not allow. The professional rules should specifically state that this behavior is unprofessional. In view of the history of this practice, it is remarkable that it is not specifically forbidden.

In Example 12 (Taking Advantage of Another Lawyer's Ignorance), a lawyer represents a party in the negotiation of a settlement of a dispute. It is apparent to the lawyer that the attorney for the opposing party is unaware of a new law that substantially strengthens the opposing party's bargaining position. The lawyer does not inform his adversary of the new law. The settlement agreement is considerably more favorable to the client of the knowledgeable lawyer than it would have been had the adversary's attorney been properly informed. The informed lawyer's conduct is permissible under the rules.

The withholding of the relevant information has the effect of achieving for the client more than the law provides. The rules explicitly forbid a lawyer to deliberately misrepresent the law;[29] exploiting the opposing attorney's ignorance in this circumstance has the same effect. The tactic harms the opposing party by denying him a benefit to which he is legally entitled. There is no consideration that justifies this harm.

The professional rules explicitly provide that a lawyer must inform a judge of legal authority (a statute or a case) known to the lawyer to be directly adverse to the position of her client and not disclosed by the opposing attorney.[30] In court the lawyer cannot take advantage of the opposing party or the judge. There should be no difference in the situation of the out-of-court settlement.

In Example 13 (Dealing with the Unrepresented Person), the lawyer represents a company selling computer programming services to commercial enterprises. The lawyer prepared a form contract with terms on copyrights, warranties, and a variety of risks that are very favorable to his client. The purchasers of the services usually retain an attorney to negotiate the terms to make them more balanced. The lawyer for the computer programming company considers his form contract to be a starting point for negotiations. Occasionally a small businessperson does not hire an attorney and signs the contract as presented to him. The lawyer assumes the businessperson does not understand the terms and how they affect him. The lawyer never advises such a person that he should hire an attorney. The lawyer's conduct is professionally proper; he has no duty to tell an unrepresented person that he should hire an attorney.

Generally speaking, the law allows the parties to arrange their contractual rights and duties as they see fit. Such is the case here. The lawyer has obtained for his client what the law allows his client. This tactic does not deceive or inflict harm. It is akin to honest bargaining in which one party obtains an advantage over another party by legally and morally permissible means. It is arguable that the moral duty of beneficence (doing of good without excessive cost to oneself) has been violated by not advising the other party to hire an attorney. This duty, however, is superseded by the lawyer's commitment to obtain for his client what the law allows. The lawyer's commitment is within the moral duty of fidelity (keeping promises).

Nevertheless, there is something unseemly about not advising the other party to hire an attorney. Some lawyers would advise the other party to hire an attorney in this circumstance; the lawyer is not required to press for every advantage that may be realized for his client,[31] and there is an aspect of unfairness here that is troubling. It seems reasonable and proper that the professional rules should provide that a lawyer must advise an unrepresented person with whom he is dealing to hire a lawyer in circumstances in which there is a substantial need. This would subordinate the client's interests to a broader social objective of fairness in transactional relationships. Such subordination seems proper for a profession.

In Example 14 (Arguing Pro and Con), the lawyer argued for a particular interpretation of a statute that was accepted by the trial judge, resulting in a victory for his client. Some months later, in a similar law suit involving different parties before a different trial judge, the same lawyer argued for an interpretation of the same statute opposite to the interpretation he had argued for in the previous suit.

This inconsistency is professionally permissible because the lawyer is the agent of the client that he is representing at the moment, dedicated exclusively to the achievement of that client's objective. Given the lawyer's role, there is no hypocrisy. The lawyer is not engaged in any deception, nor is he breaching any promise to his former client.

On the one hand, a case can be made that if the lawyer's argument prevails in the second suit, it may cause harm to his first client in some future lawsuit. On the other hand, if lawyers were precluded from making certain legal arguments because they were inconsistent with positions previously taken on behalf of other clients, lawyers' professional freedom would be severely constrained. It seems that whatever harm to the first client may result from the inconsistency, it is justified by the societal interest in the availability of legal services.

A CONTRADICTION

In Chapter 2 we examined the justification for lawyers' service on behalf of the client's legal but immoral objective. The justification is founded upon the proper functioning of our flawed but fundamentally just legal system, which requires that lawyers assist clients in realizing what the law allows even when it is immoral or socially destructive.

That same flawed but fundamentally just legal system permits or requires lawyers to employ means in their representation of clients that have the purpose or effect of impeding the realization of a result consonant with the law. This is blatantly inconsistent with the systemic justification described in the previous paragraph. The value that may be offered to support this inconsistency is zealous dedication to the interests of the client. It cannot be seriously maintained, however, that partisan loyalty transcends the proper legal result in the resolution of civil disputes. Nevertheless, a case may be made, as described above, for the moral priority of confidentiality in the representation of the criminal defendant; even here the lawyer is required to take action if his client insists upon testifying perjuriously or if the lawyer learns after his client has testified that his testimony was perjurious.

THE JUSTICE THEORY OF REPRESENTATION

The thrust of this chapter is that the means employed by lawyers in their representation of clients are often morally unjustifiable. Lawyers become acculturated to the acceptance of the "sporting theory of representation"— that is, a contest with its own rules, devoid of moral meaning. What is lost sight of is the impact of this behavior upon public confidence in our institutions, the quality of justice, and the stability of our system of freedom under law. Lawyers know that the public does not hold the profession in high esteem.[32] It is not clear, however, that the profession appreciates the relationship between the public's perception of the profession and the stability of our system of freedom under law. The system derives from the consent of the citizens. This consent is ultimately dependent upon the belief that, in general, the system operates fairly. It belabors the obvious to state that the behavior of lawyers affects the perception of the fairness of the system as well as the fairness itself.

It is suggested that the sporting theory of representation should be replaced by a "justice theory of representation." The lawyer's role should be to achieve for the client only what the facts allow him under the law. The lawyer as zealous advocate should be replaced by the lawyer as an instrument of justice. It is not suggested that the adversarial method be abandoned, but rather that it be limited to honest differences concerning facts and law. This is not pie-in-the-sky academic idealism. Many lawyers practice in this fashion, and there has been a recent procedural development in the federal courts that leans in that direction. This is the subject of the next section.

One might object that this proposed change in the role of the lawyer would affect fundamentally the lawyer's relationship of loyalty to the client. This relationship, however, is a qualified one even under the existing rules. There are duties to the court in a trial that take precedence over the duties of confidentiality and loyalty owed to the client. The lawyer may divulge confidences to protect his own interests in various circumstances. The lawyer is free to disclose the client's intention to commit a crime. The lawyer is not required to press for an advantage that may be realized for his client where such advantage would be deemed to be unfair by the lawyer.

The proposed change would make the lawyer's duty to his client coextensive with what he is entitled to under the law. Why should a client expect more? Why should a profession provide more?

An Experiment

As of December 1, 1993, a procedural rule came into effect in the federal trial courts in civil (not criminal) litigation that requires each party prior to the trial to disclose to the opposition the names of all persons who have information relevant to the law suit, the nature of the information, and the identity of all documents and physical evidence relevant to the suit in the party's possession or control.[33] The purpose is to provide the parties with all the information then known that bears on the law suit. Truth in litigation is the objective. This is a striking and controversial departure from past practice. Some background is required to appreciate fully this development.

Until sixty years ago, in federal and most state trial courts, there was no legal procedure before the trial began to determine the nature of the evidence that the other side was going to present. The only disclosure was what appeared in the pleadings; that is, the plaintiff's complaint and the defendant's answer to it. Each party tried to find out before trial what they could about the opposition's evidence through private investigation, which often was fragmentary and inadequate. At the trial, when one party presented his witnesses and other evidence, the opposing attorney countered it as best he could through cross-examination or the presentation of conflicting evidence that he was able to uncover. The attorneys were often confronted with evidence that was unanticipated. The element of surprise was characteristic. It was often impossible to prepare adequately for trial.[34] Truth was the victim.

In 1938 the federal courts adopted rules to correct this situation by providing legal procedures for discovering, outside of court and before trial, the nature of the adversary's evidence. The attorney for a party could require the opposing party, or anyone else having information concerning the subject of the suit, to respond orally under oath to questions, of which a transcript is made. This is called a "deposition." One party may require the other party to respond in writing under oath to written questions sent to him concerning matters relevant to the suit. These are called "interrogatories." In addition, one party may require the other party, or a third person, to produce documents and other property in its possession or control that are relevant to the suit for inspection and copying. These procedures are collectively referred to as "discovery."[35]

State courts have adopted the same or similar rules. They are designed to enable the parties to prepare their cases adequately, to avoid surprise at the trial, and to facilitate the resolution of the dispute at trial on the basis of the truth. In addition, the availability of such information before trial increases substantially the likelihood of a settlement that is preferable to the expense and unpleasantness of a trial. However, the proverbial "smoking gun"—evidence that is critically damaging to the opponent's case—sometimes is not discovered because the right question is not asked, or at least is not asked with the requisite specificity.

Discovery functioned as it was intended for several decades. By the 1970s, however, the discovery process was frequently being used for purposes that were never intended.[36] Depositions, interrogatories, and document production involve costs in the form of clients' time, witnesses' time, and lawyers' time. If employed excessively, as they often were, the process can be very expensive and burdensome. Legal objections to the relevance or scope of depositions, interrogatories, and demands for documents, which require judicial attention, are also expensive. The process that was designed to facilitate efficient justice was often transformed into a tactic of pre-trial adversary conflict, the object of which was to wear down the opponent, particularly if the opponent had limited resources. Lawyers beat the ploughshare into a sword. The cost of litigation often was enormously increased by the tactical abuse of the discovery process, and the resolution of disputes often was distorted by the use, or the fear of the use, of this new weapon in the arsenal of the aggressive trial lawyer. Lawyers attempted to justify these tactics as zealous advocacy.

The games played in the discovery process are numerous.[37] For example, the party seeking information may make demands that are extremely broad, sometimes referred to as a "fishing expedition." The purpose of such an expedition may be to find evidence for new claims other than those in dispute, to uncover business secrets, or simply to harass. In response to a demand for documents of a certain nature, a lawyer may include a mass of marginally relevant or irrelevant documents together with the significant documents, making it costly for the other party to uncover the significant information. Yet another abusive practice is the use of very lengthy oral depositions, which can also be costly. The purpose of a deposition is to discover information from the opposing party or a witness for the opposing party. It is necessary for the attorney for the party being deposed to be present to object to improper questions or other forms of abuse of the deponent. Attorney costs, of course, can be great. Extended depositions can also disrupt the deponent's personal life and business.

The American Bar Association summarized the problems of discovery in a 1986 report:

> Discovery is one of the principal areas in which problems arise in litigation. Particularly in complex cases, litigation no longer means merely trials, but often months or years of pretrial process. Massive amounts of material are often demanded so that the costs of production will be high. Excessive amounts of material are often delivered so that the costs of examination will be prohibitive. Hypertechnical interpretations of discovery requests are made so as to withhold documents.[38]

These problems caused the federal courts to adopt a rule, effective December 1, 1993, that each party before trial must disclose to the other party, without being asked, the names of all individuals known to have information relevant to the lawsuit and the nature of the information, as well as the identity of all documents and physical evidence relevant to the suit in the party's possession or control.[39] The information to be provided includes that which is favorable to a party as well as that which is unfavorable. Any "smoking gun" evidence must be disclosed.

The purpose of the new rule is to provide the sum of all information available that is relevant to the suit right at the outset. It is reiterated that this is mandatory disclosure without request. This is the same information that ideally would be made available upon request under the discovery process, without the expense, quibbling, obfuscation, and evasiveness of that process. After such mandatory disclosure, the conventional discovery process would be available, but it would be greatly simplified. The witnesses and the documents would already have been identified. The new rule was intended to make the truth more accessible at greatly reduced cost. Each federal trial court was allowed to opt out of the new rule; one-half have done so.[40]

It should be emphasized that the new procedure runs counter to the instincts of the lawyer in the adversary system of justice. The lawyer must voluntarily disclose information to the opposition that is damaging to his client's case. It is one thing to be required to respond to a specific request from one's opponent; it is another to come forth with such damaging information on one's own. This may be perceived as a form of disloyalty by both lawyer and client. In the hearings that were held prior to the adoption of the rule, the opposition to it was widespread among most elements of the bar.[41]

The procedural rules governing the federal courts are adopted by the United States Supreme Court. With respect to this rule, the Supreme Court was divided. Justices Scalia, Souter, and Thomas dissented, stating, in part, as follows:

> The proposed new regime does not fit comfortably within the American judicial system, which relies on adversarial litigation to develop the facts before a neutral decision maker. By placing upon lawyers the obligation to disclose information damaging to their clients—on their own initiative, and in a context where the lines between what must be disclosed and what need not be disclosed are not clear but require the exercise of considerable judgment—the new Rule would place intolerable strain upon lawyers' ethical duty to represent their clients and not to assist the opposing side. Requiring a lawyer to make a judgment as to what information is "relevant to disputed facts" plainly requires him to use his professional skills in the service of the adversary.[42]

Griffin Bell, formerly Attorney General in the Carter administration and a Federal Appeals Court judge, also opposed the new rule when it was being proposed:

> Under the current federal rules of discovery, the obligation is on the requesting party to identify with some degree of specificity those documents the party needs to make out a case. In contrast, under an automatic disclosure requirement, the responding party and his or her attorney will be required to determine unilaterally the categories of information they believe the opponent will need to pursue his or her claims or defenses. Therefore, the responding party will have to stand in the shoes of the adversary, visualizing the types of documents and information that the adversary may need.
>
> As a result, the proposed rule may well reverse the roles of plaintiffs and defendants. For example, . . . a defendant will have to analyze the nature of the plaintiff's claim and decide what types of documents and information will be needed to prove the case. Critics have charged that, in essence, the defendant will be required to assist in making the plaintiff's case for the plaintiff. This result clearly would be contrary to the traditional notions of the lawyer's role.
> . . .[43]

It is apparent that modification of the traditional adversarial posture of the lawyer is not received well even at the highest levels of the profession. Cultural change does not come easily.

Others have maintained that mandatory disclosure will be transformed into gamesmanship in the same manner as the conventional discovery process. The information that is to be disclosed is that which is "relevant to disputed facts alleged with particularity." Lawyers will quarrel over what is "relevant," what facts are "disputed," and whether the disputed facts are alleged with "particularity," and apply to the judge for the resolution of these questions. If lawyers continue to act like lawyers, there will be expense and delay as in conventional discovery. After this hassle, the lawyers are free to use conventional discovery to make sure that everything that was supposed to be disclosed under mandatory disclosure has been disclosed. All that would be accomplished would be the addition of another layer of controversy.[44]

Another commentator saw the promulgation of mandatory disclosure as the "triumph of hope over experience:"

> The movement for promulgation of a mandatory informal discovery rule is based on at least two assumptions. The first assumption is that the current civil discovery rules are ineffective and counterproductive to their intended ends. Thus, rather than promoting free and liberal discovery of information about a case, contemporary federal practice instead encourages gamesmanship. Not only does this violate the spirit of the 1938 discovery provisions, but it frustrates the stated goals of the rules of procedure by encouraging injustice, delay, and needless expense.
>
> The second assumption underlying an informal discovery rule is that such a rule somehow will help to cure prevailing discovery ills. In this regard, the Advisory Committee is demonstrating the triumph of hope over experience. Of all the rules of civil procedure, the various discovery provisions have been amended most frequently. No matter how many times the Advisory Committee redrafts the discovery rules, discovery abuse continues unabated, as lawyers create new ways to circumvent the rules. Only an Advisory Committee with an aspirational vision of professional conduct could hope that a new mandatory informal discovery provision will succeed where previous discovery reforms have failed to modify abusive lawyering tactics.[45]

The justice theory of representation means that the lawyer's obligation should be to achieve for the client what the law allows and no more. Mandatory disclosure, in its design and purpose, is a significant step in that direction; it may, of course, be sabotaged by commonplace tactics of lawyers. It is limited to specific conduct in the litigation setting. The justice theory of representation applies to all conduct, not only in the litigation context but also in the settlement of disputes, negotiation, investigation, preparation of documents, and so on.

It will take time to determine whether mandatory disclosure will fall victim to the adversarial spirit and thereby fail to achieve its purpose. If that occurs it will establish that well-intentioned procedures cannot do the job of correcting what is wrong with the behavior of lawyers. The root of the problem is in the professional rules that do not require truth-seeking and justice-seeking, but only proscribe fraud, lying, and criminality. As long as the constraints are as limited as they are, and the duty is perceived to be to achieve for the client whatever one can within the professional rules, little change is likely to occur.

Twenty years ago, Marvin Frankel—a prominent commentator on the profession, former professor of law at Columbia, and former federal trial court judge—advocated that the professional rules should be amended to provide that it is the duty of the lawyer representing a party in a lawsuit to "report to the court and opposing counsel the existence of relevant evidence or witnesses where the lawyer does not intend to offer such evidence or witness." He also advocated that the lawyer should be required to report to the court and opposing counsel any omission by a witness of a "material fact necessary in order to make statements made . . . not misleading." He criticized the professional rules for merely proscribing "positive frauds," rather than mandating truth-seeking.[46]

Frankel's proposal for changes in the professional rules applies the justice theory of representation to the litigation setting. Analogous truth-seeking and justice-seeking should be extended to all areas of practice. Only then will the lawyer be dedicated to achieving what the law allows his client, no more and no less.

The professional rules, of course, will not be changed unless the adversarial culture of the profession is changed. In the professional culture, the highest value is the achievement of the client's objective, whether or not it is consonant with truth and justice. Certainly a profession that includes some of the best minds in our society should aim for something better.

Notes

1. Among state courts the prevailing position is that the judiciary has the inherent power to regulate the profession, to the exclusion of the legislature. On the other hand, it is clear that in the federal system Congress has the power to regulate the profession. Charles W. Wolfram, Modern Legal Ethics 22–33 (West, 1986).

2. Fifth and Fourteenth Amendments to the United States Constitution. Wayne R. La Fave and Jerold Israel, Criminal Procedure 448 (West, 2d. ed., 1992).

3. For a discussion of this privilege, see Charles W. Wolfram, Modern Legal Ethics 250–291 (West 1986).

4. McCormick on Evidence 141, 109, 112 (John W. Strong ed., West, 4th ed., 1992).

5. Fourth and Fourteenth Amendments to the United States Constitution, Wayne R. La Fave and Jerold Israel, Criminal Procedure 105 (West, 2d. ed., 1992).

6. Marvin E. Frankel, The Search for Truth: An Umpireal View, 123 *University of Pennsylvania Law Review* 1031, 1036 (1975).

7. Monroe H. Freedman, Judge Frankel's Search for Truth, 123 *University of Pennsylvania Law Review* 1060 (1975). Freedman has expanded and updated his analysis in M. H. Freedman, Understanding Lawyer's Ethics, Ch. 2 (Matthew Bender, 1990).

8. Richard Wasserstrom, Lawyers as Professionals: Some Moral Issues, 5 Human Rights 13 (1975). Permission to reprint granted by the American Bar Association, the Section of Individual Rights and Responsibilities, and Southern Methodist University.

9. Model Rule 1.6(a).

10. This quote is from Rule 4-101(c)(3) of the 1969 Model Code of Professional Responsibility. Model Rule 1.6(b) of the 1983 Model Rules of Professional Conduct limits disclosure of intended crimes to those likely to result in imminent death or substantial bodily harm. Although a large majority of states have adopted generally the 1983 Model Rules, many of these states modified the disclosure provision concerning intended crimes to include all crimes. A majority of states permit disclosure of any intended crime regardless of its nature.

11. Model Rule 1.6(b)(2).

12. Model Rule 3.3(a)(4), Comment.

13. Rule 3.3(a)(2), Comment.

14. Monroe H. Freedman, Understanding Lawyers' Ethics 111–120 (Matthew Bender, 1990).

15. Model Rule 1.2(d).

16. Only four states have statutes making it a misdemeanor for one to fail to aid someone in peril if there is no risk to oneself. Nowhere is civil liability imposed. It should be emphasized that if a person has assumed responsibility, such as a baby-sitter, failure to act would result in civil and possibly criminal liability.

17. There has been considerable discussion on the subject of the duty to rescue in the academic journals in recent years. E.g., Mary Ann Glendon, Does the United States Need "Good Samaritan" Laws? 1 *Responsive Community* 9 (1991); Steven J. Heyman, Foundations of the Duty to Rescue, 47 *Vanderbilt Law Review* 673 (1994); Joel Feinberg, The Moral and Legal Responsibility of the Bad Samaritan, 3 *Criminal Justice Ethics* 56 (1984); Ernest J. Weinrib, The Case for a Duty to Rescue, 90 *Yale Law Journal* 247 (1980).

18. Restatement 2d of Contracts §161 (1981); Restatement 2d of Torts §551 (1977).

19. E. Allan Farnsworth, Contracts §4.11 (Little, Brown, 1990); William L. Prosser and W. Page Keeton, Law of Torts §106 (West, 5th ed., 1984).

20. Model Rule 3.3(a)(4).

21. For discussions supporting limitations on criminal defense tactics, see Harry I. Subin, The Criminal Lawyer's "Different Mission": Reflections on the "Right" to Present a False Case, 1 *Georgetown Journal of Legal Ethics* 125 (1987); William H. Simon, The Ethics of Criminal Defense, 91 *Michigan Law Review* 1703 (1993).

22. Model Rule 1.2(d).

23. Model Rule 4.1(a).

24. Model Rule 4.1, Comment 2.

25. For a thorough discussion of negotiation issues, see Charles W. Wolfram, Modern Legal Ethics 710 (West, 1986).

26. Model Rule 1.2(d).

27. Model Rule 8.4(c).

28. Robert E. Keeton, Trial Tactics and Methods §9.12 (Little, Brown, 2d ed., 1973).

29. Rule 4.1(a).

30. Model Rule 3.3(a)(3).

31. Model Rule 1.3, Comment.

32. Chapter VI of an American Bar Association study entitled Lawyer Advertising at the Crossroads (1995) discusses the public's attitude towards the profession,

which, in general, is not favorable. One survey found that the public's attitude towards physicians, dentists, and CPAs was much more favorable than its attitude towards lawyers and that insurance agents were viewed slightly more favorably than lawyers.

33. Rule 26 of the Federal Rules of Civil Procedure.

34. Jack H. Friedenthal, Mary Kay Kane, and Arthur R. Miller, Civil Procedure 379 (West, 2d ed., 1993).

35. *Id.* at 395–412.

36. William W. Schwarzer, The Federal Rules, The Adversary Process, and Discovery Reform, 50 *University of Pittsburgh Law Review* 703 (1989).

37. Wayne D. Brazil, The Adversary Character of Civil Discovery: A Critique and Proposals for Change, 31 *Vanderbilt Law Review* 1295, 1315 (1978); Virginia E. Hench, Mandatory Disclosure and Equal Access to Justice: The 1993 Federal Discovery Rules Amendment and the Just, Speedy and Inexpensive Determination of Every Action, 67 *Temple Law Review* 179, 209–219 (1994); Senate Report No. 101–416, Judicial Improvements Act of 1990, in 1990 *U.S. Code Congressional and Administrative News* 6802, 6823.

38. In the Spirit of Public Service: A Blueprint for the Rekindling of Lawyer Professionalism 29 (1986). This is a report on the state of the profession by the American Bar Association.

39. Rule 26 of the Federal Rules of Civil Procedure.

40. Ashley C. Belleau, A Critique of the "New" Discovery Rules, 42 *Federal Lawyer* 36 (July 1995).

41. William D. Bertelsman, Changing the Rules of Pretrial Fact Disclosure, 46 *Florida Law Review* 105 (1994); Griffin Bell, Chilton Davis Varner, and Hugh Q. Gottschalk, Automatic Disclosure in Discovery—The Rush to Reform, 27 *Georgia Law Review* 1,3 (1992); Dissenting Statement of Justices Scalia, Thomas, and Souter, 146 *Federal Rules Decisions* 512 (1993).

42. Dissenting Statement of Justices Scalia, Thomas, and Souter, 146 *Federal Rules Decisions* 511 (1993).

43. Griffin Bell, Chilton Davis Varner, and Hugh Q. Gottschalk, Automatic Disclosure in Discovery—The Rush to Reform, 27 *Georgia Law Review* 47 (1992).

44. Id. at 40; Virginia E. Hench, Mandatory Disclosure and Equal Access to Justice: The 1993 Federal Discovery Rules Amendments and the Just, Speedy and Inexpensive Determination of Every Action, 67 *Temple Law Review* 179, 206 (1994); Dissenting Statement of Justices Scalia, Thomas, and Souter, 146 *Federal Rules Decisions* 510 (1993).

45. Linda S. Mullenix, Hope Over Experience: Mandatory Informal Discovery and the Politics of Rulemaking, 69 *North Carolina Law Review* 795, 820 (1991).

46. Marvin E. Frankel, The Search for Truth: An Umpireal View, 123 *University of Pennsylvania Law Review* 1031, 1057 (1975).

4

A Troubled Profession

There is a perception among many in the profession that the behavior of lawyers has changed for the worse recently. This is not because more lawyers are violating the letter of the rules than in the past. Rather it appears that more lawyers are practicing in a manner that displays a callous disregard for the interests of others. The profession has become more competitive and acquisitive, causing lawyers to be more aggressive and less civil. In this chapter we examine these contemporary circumstances.

The Hired Gun and the Independent Lawyer

The theory of "role morality," discussed in Chapter 2, allows the lawyer to do for his client what he would not be morally permitted to do for himself. The legally permissible but morally offensive conduct is the client's, not the lawyer's; the lawyer is merely performing a role in our system of freedom under law, which permits such conduct. The executive branch, the legislature, and the courts decide what may or may not be done. The lawyer is absolved of moral responsibility in the performance of his role. Most in the profession accept this, but not all. Those who accept it do not necessarily do so comfortably or practice accordingly. As one commentator has concluded, the lawyer who practices in accordance with this view "can be a good person; not comfortable, but good."[1]

The uneasiness within the profession has been evident throughout our history. It is reflected in the professional literature by the portrayals of two models of lawyering. One is the lawyer who unquestioningly accepts the client's objective and in its pursuit zealously employs the arsenal of tactics within the law and the professional rules, regardless of the harm inflicted upon specific others or the social consequences. In contemporary parlance this model is often disparagingly referred to as the "hired gun." It has been neutrally described as the "total commitment" model.[2]

The other model is the lawyer who in his counseling and representation exercises independent judgment in his relationship to the client. This lawyer, in his advice, provides the client the benefit of his judgment of the prudence, long-term consequences, morality, and social responsibility of the client's objective and of the tactics and strategies for its accomplishment. If the lawyer's judgment is that they, or any of them, are unworthy, and if the client is unconvinced that he should refrain, the lawyer may decline or terminate the representation. This model is sometimes referred to as the "independent lawyer."[3]

The professional rules permit the lawyer to practice in accordance with the hired gun model or the independent lawyer model, as he chooses. Much of the conduct described in the examples in Chapter 1 is illustrative of the hired gun. It was noted there that many lawyers would refrain from certain tactics or decline or terminate the representation in certain circumstances. The rules provide that the lawyer need not "press for every advantage that might be realized for a client."[4] The rules permit the lawyer to decline representation at his discretion and to terminate representation if the client insists upon pursuing an objective that the lawyer considers "repugnant or imprudent."[5] The rules also refer to the value of incorporating moral and social considerations in the advice to clients.[6] It is fair to say that the rules encourage the lawyer to practice in accordance with the independent lawyer model.

It is generally accepted that in recent decades the hired gun model has become predominant.[7] There are no statistics on the subject, but there seems to be a consensus in the profession that there are more lawyers who practice in that style today than did forty or fifty years ago and that the style has become more aggressive than in the past. When lawyers speak of the decline of professionalism today, it is this shift in professional behavior together with a breakdown in civility among lawyers; the introduction of advertising, marketing, and solicitation of legal business; and the emphasis upon the financial "bottom line" that are typically referred to. The practice of law has become more competitive and commercialized.

In the nineteenth century there were two prominent lecturers and essayists in the field of legal ethics, George Sharswood and David Hoffman. The tension between the two styles of lawyering was apparent in their presentations. In his Essay on Professional Ethics, first published in 1854, George Sharswood appears to make the case for one position, but later, in a contradictory statement, argues for the other position. First, this:

> The party has a right to have his case decided upon the law and the evidence, and to have every view presented to the minds of the judges, which can legitimately bear upon the question. This is the office which the advocate performs. He is not morally responsible for the act of the party in maintaining an unjust cause, nor for the error of the court, if they fall into error, in deciding it in his favor. The court or jury ought certainly to hear and weigh both sides; and the

office of the counsel is to assist them by doing that, which the client in person, from want of learning, experience, and address, is unable to do in a proper manner. The lawyer, who refuses his professional assistance because in his judgment the case is unjust and indefensible, usurps the functions of both judge and jury.[8]

Then this:

Counsel have an undoubted right, and are in duty bound, to refuse to be concerned for a plaintiff in the legal pursuit of a demand, which offends his sense of what is just and right. The courts are open to the party in person to prosecute his own claim, and plead his own cause; and although he ought to examine and be well satisfied before he refuses to a suitor the benefit of his professional skill and learning, yet it would be on his part an immoral act to afford that assistance, when his conscience told him that the client was aiming to perpetrate a wrong through the means of some advantage the law may have afforded him.[9]

David Hoffman, in his essay entitled Resolutions in Regard to Professional Deportment, published in 1839, is adamant in his opposition to the hired gun model:

If, after duly examining a case, I am persuaded that my client's claim or defense (as the case may be,) cannot, or rather ought not, to be sustained, I will promptly advise him to abandon it. To press it further in such a case, with the hope of gleaning some advantage by an extorted compromise, would be lending myself to a dishonourable use of legal means, in order to gain a *portion* of that, the *whole* of which I have reason to believe would be denied to him both by law and justice.

I will never plead the Statute of Limitations, when based on the *mere efflux of time*; for if my client is conscious he owes the debt; and has no other defense than the *legal bar*, he shall never make me a partner in his knavery.[10]

Abraham Lincoln also weighed in on the side of professional independence in his advice to a client:

Yes, we can doubtless gain your case for you; we can set a whole neighborhood at loggerheads; we can distress a widowed mother and her six fatherless children and thereby get you six hundred dollars to which you seem to have a legal claim, but which rightfully belongs, it appears to me, as much to the woman and her children as it does to you. You must remember that some things legally right are not morally right. We shall not take your case, but will give you a little advice for which we will charge you nothing. You seem to be a sprightly, energetic man; we would advise you to try your hand at making six hundred dollars in some other way.[11]

In the early years of this century a shift in the style of lawyering among the elite of the profession was recognized by two prominent members of the profession, Louis Brandeis and Woodrow Wilson. First, Brandeis:

It is true that at the present time the lawyer does not hold as high a position with the people as he held seventy-five or indeed fifty years ago; but the reason is not lack of opportunity. It is this: Instead of holding a position of independence, between the wealthy and the people, prepared to curb the excesses of either, lawyers have, to a large extent, allowed themselves to become adjuncts of great corporations and have neglected the obligation to use their powers for the protection of the people. . . . . [12]

Next, Wilson:

A new type of lawyer has been created; and that new type has come to be the prevailing type. Lawyers have been sucked into the maelstrom of the new business system of the country. That system is highly technical and highly specialized. . . . [Lawyers] do not handle the general, miscellaneous interests of society. They are not general counselors of right and obligation. They do not bear the relation to the business of their neighborhoods that the family doctor bears to the health of the community in which he lives. They do not concern themselves with the universal aspects of society. . . . [13]

In the face of the prevailing acceptance of the hired gun style of lawyering in recent years, contemporary commentators on the condition of the profession have spoken of the need to preserve the independence of lawyers. Archibald Cox, former professor of law at Harvard, Solicitor General of the United States, and Watergate prosecutor, had this to say:

The "independent lawyer" develops the capacity for taking a longer and broader view than the first look of many clients engaged in pressing immediate self-advantage.

. . .

Independence frees the lawyer from the emotional involvement and short-run material self-interest that confuse judgment. The independent lawyer looks not only to what the client thinks it wants but to the interests of others whom the client's action will affect, including the larger, undifferentiated interests of the general public. In this there is no real ambivalence. With the larger consequences before it, the client may perceive that its true long-range goals are bound up with standards of decency and with the welfare not only of the other parties to the immediate controversy but of wider segments of society. With the larger consequences before it, the client may change its view of what it wants; it may separate out the main objective, thereby eliminating cause for controversy or harm to others; or it may pursue the same goal by a different method that avoids or reduces injury to others.[14]

Roger Cramton, former dean of Cornell Law School and present member of the faculty and an authority on professional ethics, has commented on the contemporary reasons for the hired gun style:

Is today's lawyer a buffer between the illegitimate or immoral desires of clients and the public interest? Or is he the amoral facilitator of the client's selfish goals? . . . The hired-gun mentality is convenient, profitable, and finds increasing support in the profession's own ideology.

It is unnecessary here to delineate all of the structural and economic circumstances that push toward the hired-gun mentality. The increasing specialization of the bar has dissolved collegial ties and relates each lawyer, not to the profession at large, but to clients with a particular interest. The increasing competition for legal work, the growth in the size of organizations in which law practice is carried on, the assertion of control over legal work by corporate clients, and the tendency of lawyers to identify with the views and interests of their clients all tend to make lawyers dependent upon clients rather than a possible moral influence on them.

. . .

When corporate lawyers get together today, the talk is not of the plight of legal services for the poor or law reform, but of ways of hustling for clients—marketing plans, seminars for new clients, public-relations brochures and blitzes. Instead of talking about the personal responsibility of a lawyer for a client, the talk is of top-down and outside control of legal work.[15]

It seems that independent lawyering would be most feasible for large elite law firms serving national corporations, because of such firms' prosperity, status, and security. As the words of Brandeis and Wilson indicate, however, it appears that in the past at least some of them have been merely servants of corporate interests. In recent years there has been a change in the nature of law practice at this level that makes independent lawyering more difficult than ever. Roger Cramton's comments described the contemporary situation in summary fashion. The change that has taken place has been in process for about three decades.

Forty years ago large corporations typically had a handful of lawyer-employees whose roles were usually limited to routine functions such as minor contract negotiations. The corporation retained a large law firm in a major city to handle significant legal problems. The firm usually bore the title of "general counsel" to the corporation. It was staffed to furnish most of the legal services the corporation required, such as tax, securities, finance, real estate, corporate administration, trade regulation, and major litigation. Minor litigation, which might occur in a variety of places, was farmed out to local attorneys whose activities were overseen by the general counsel.

Although many lawyers in the firm worked on the corporation's matters, usually there was one senior partner in the firm who oversaw the performance of the legal services and to whom the senior corporate officers turned for advice and guidance. The relationship between the corporation and the firm often was long-term, lasting for decades. Usually, the firm was sufficiently secure in its relationship to exercise a substantial degree of independence, if it chose to do so. If the firm's legal judgment on a matter was not what the client wanted to hear, the client was unlikely to shop around for another law firm that would tell it what it wanted to hear.[16]

The world of law became more complex in the 1970s and 1980s due to the internationalization of commerce, new forms of governmental regulation of commerce, the explosion of the grounds for lawsuits recognized by courts, and the increased inclination of individuals and corporations to resort to law to resolve disputes. Legal expenses skyrocketed, and many large corporations responded by greatly expanding their in-house legal departments to handle less expensively many matters that previously were referred to the law firm serving as general counsel.[17]

Prior to this expansion, "house counsel" employment did not enjoy the status of private firm employment and did not offer the potential for financial rewards of private employment. With the expansion, status and compensation have been enhanced significantly. Often the vice-president in charge of the corporate legal department carries the title of general counsel, replacing in function and status the senior partner of the law firm in prior years. The credentials of the lawyers on the corporate staff are often comparable to those of lawyers in the large law firms.[18]

The development of the in-house legal staff has, of course, transformed the role of the law firm servicing the corporation. Instead of handling generally the legal matters of the corporation, the law firm is hired to perform certain legal tasks for which the in-house staff is not qualified, for which it needs assistance, or for which outside counsel is otherwise required. For example, the in-house staff may not have the manpower to handle complex, protracted litigation, or it may not have anyone knowledgeable in a specialized area of taxation, securities regulation, or intellectual property. Sometimes bargaining and negotiations are best conducted by outside counsel; opinions and certifications of outside counsel may be required by third parties.[19]

Typically the corporation does not send all of its outside work to one large law firm. The increased cost-consciousness of the corporation dictates that it obtain the required services at the lowest price available from qualified law firms. Firms are invited to make presentations to the head of the corporate legal department concerning their qualifications and their fees or hourly rates for the job. This practice is sometimes referred to in the trade as a "beauty contest."[20]

For the most part, the "general counsel" law firm, with its institutionalized, long-term relationship to the corporate client, is a thing of the past. Firms now compete for specific jobs from corporations. This competition has produced a practice known as "marketing," a form of nonpublic advertising. The law firm sends potential corporate clients glossy brochures portraying the qualifications of its lawyers and the range of services it is capable of providing. It distributes newsletters describing recent developments in the law and suggesting law-related strategies that clients may wish to pursue. The firm invites potential clients to seminars conducted by firm lawyers on a variety of legal topics. Outings are held for clients at comfortable country clubs. Lawyers who specialize in suing on behalf of individuals who have been injured advertise on television and send letters to accident victims; law firms that do corporate work use other techniques because their potential clients are identifiable.[21]

The hired gun accepts unquestioningly what the client wants to do and employs all legal means to achieve it. The independent lawyer adopts the role of the uninvolved counselor who provides an objective perspective upon the means and ends that the client proposes; there may be long-term consequences to the client or social or moral consequences that the client does not perceive in his quest for immediate gain. The hired gun puts on blinders. The independent lawyer critically examines the client's situation in the interest of the client.

Is it likely that the lawyer who aggressively pursues business through marketing techniques and competes for work put out to bid by corporations is going to adopt the role of the independent lawyer? Maybe, but not likely. The lawyer can afford to adopt that role when he is respected by the client and secure in his relationship. The client's visceral reaction to independent advice may not be favorable. The lawyer who has obtained work through a competitive process in which he has bested other qualified lawyers is not likely to be inclined to tell the client what he prefers not to hear. The hired gun model is better suited to this circumstance.[22]

Now that the corporate executive—that is, the vice president and general counsel—is in charge, maybe he provides the independent advice. He is a part of a management team, however, and is involved on a regular basis with those designing business strategy. He is also an employee of the corporation and a subordinate to the president, executive vice-president, and directors of the corporation. These factors are not conducive to independent lawyering. It may be that the chief lawyer in the corporation is an independent counselor, but one's intuition is that it is unlikely.[23]

The phenomenon of law firms competing for business from corporations has produced a professional atmosphere of insecurity and fluidity that was unknown several decades ago. In the past the career pattern for the law school graduate who joined the large firm was well-defined. In the first five to ten years, depending on the firm, he worked as an associate—that is, as an employee. A minor fraction of associates who were hired were selected for partnership. The partner would remain in the firm until retirement.

It was unusual for a partner to leave the firm to practice with another firm or to join a corporation. The associate who was not selected for partnership would often leave to join another firm, usually smaller and less prestigious, or a corporate staff. It was unusual for an associate to move from one large firm to another. Large corporate firms rarely dissolved into separate firms as a result of personal differences or business circumstances.[24]

All of this has changed. The intense competition among law firms causes business to move from one to another. Correspondingly, associates and partners move from one firm to another. An entire department specializing in a particular area may break off and form its own firm of specialists. Firms merge with one another as business needs require and dissolve into separate entities as business circumstances change. Today, the career pattern for the law graduate who joins the large firm is unpredictable. Insecurity and fluidity have replaced stability and status in the world of corporate law practice.[25]

So far we have focused on an extremely influential but minor fraction of the bar. The majority of lawyers are engaged in a variety of other forms of practice. Some are employed in government at the municipal, state, or federal level. Others practice alone or in small firms in both large and small communities, serving local business and individuals. Real estate, decedents' estates, divorce, personal injury litigation, criminal defense, income taxation, contract drafting and negotiation, and bankruptcy constitute a substantial portion of the practice of sole practitioners and small firms everywhere.

Sole practitioner and small-firm practice representing individuals and small business is extremely diverse; generalizations about the relationship between lawyer and client in terms of the lawyer's independence or subservience to the client's objectives are conjectural. Nonetheless, it appears that the competitive spirit among lawyers in this area of practice is greater than in the past. The likelihood is that independence suffers in this climate. Certainly, the impression is widespread that the hired gun model is doing well.

ADVERTISING

The aggressive pursuit of business is of the essence of the free enterprise system. Such behavior, however, has been considered to be inappropriate for lawyers. The practice of law, it has been said, is not a trade but rather a public service by which the lawyer earns his living.[26] The lawyer is a fiduciary for the client, selflessly dedicated to the realization of the client's interests under the law. The lawyer's objective is not to maximize his income but to serve the client effectively and efficiently. The aggressive pursuit of business through advertising has been assumed to be in conflict with the spirit of the profession.

This attitude towards advertising has been a part of the professional ideology for many decades and remains so for many lawyers, but in recent years it has been disputed by a substantial portion of the profession, most significantly by a majority of the justices of the United States Supreme Court. The opposition to advertising is a twentieth-century phenomenon. Lawyers placed ads in newspapers in the 1800s without professional criticism. Abraham Lincoln advertised. The ads of that period were simple and dignified, identifying the firm and the type of practice in which it engaged.[27] The professional ideology of the time was that law practice was distinguishable from trade, but advertising in that form apparently was not considered to be in conflict with that ideal. The attitude towards advertising changed around the turn of the century. The reasons for the shift are not clear, but it has been suggested that it was related to the massive immigration of that period.[28] The homogeneity of the profession was threatened by new arrivals from southern and eastern Europe. A prohibition upon advertising would impede access to the professional market. The putative nexus between the prohibition and immigration is conjectural, but plausible.

The first body of professional standards that was national in scope was promulgated by the American Bar Association in 1908—the Canons of Professional Ethics. The American Bar Association is a nongovernmental entity whose actions have no legal effect. The Canons constituted a recommendation to the individual states, which established the professional rules of conduct. Many states formally adopted the Canons and others used the Canons as their guide in the imposition of professional discipline upon lawyers.[29]

Canon 27, which prohibited advertising, read in part as follows:

> It is unprofessional to solicit professional employment by circulars, advertisements, through touters or by personal communications or interviews not warranted by personal relations. Indirect advertisements for professional employment such as furnishing or inspiring newspaper comments, or procuring his photograph to be published in connection with causes in which the lawyer has been or is engaged or concerning the manner of their conduct, the magnitude of the interest involved, the importance of the lawyer's position, and all other like self-laudation, offend the traditions and lower the tone of our profession and are reprehensible; but the customary use of simple professional cards is not improper.

In 1969 the American Bar Association replaced the Canons with the Model Code of Professional Responsibility. The prohibition upon advertising remained. Almost all states formally adopted the 1969 Model Code or its substantial equivalent.[30]

Prior to 1976 the United States Supreme Court did not apply First Amendment protection to commercial speech, although it applied to all other areas of expression—political, social, religious, literary, scientific, and artistic. In 1976 the Court reversed its course in a decision that invalidated a Virginia statute barring pharmacists from advertising prescription drug prices as a violation of the First Amendment's guarantee of freedom of speech.[31] The Court's opinion expressly stated that this decision was not to be construed as protecting advertising by physicians or lawyers, but only a year later, in a decision in which five justices joined and four dissented, the Court held that lawyer advertising was also constitutionally protected.

In that case, *Bates v. State Bar of Arizona*,[32] a law firm placed an advertisement in a Phoenix newspaper stating fees for several routine legal services. For example, "Divorce or legal separation—uncontested . . . $175 plus $20 court filing fee," and "Bankruptcy—non-business, no contested proceedings . . . $250 plus $55 court filing fee." The lawyers were censured by the Arizona Supreme Court for violating the professional rules restricting advertising. The U.S. Supreme Court held that the advertisement was truthful and not misleading and as such was protected speech under the First Amendment. The Court noted that advertising that was false, deceptive, or misleading would *not* be protected and could be restrained by the states. As an example, the Court mentioned that advertising claims as to quality of legal services are not susceptible to measurement and would likely be considered misleading. The Court also pointed out that "special problems of advertising in the electronic broadcast media will warrant special consideration."[33] The Court stated that it was not passing judgment on the question of in-person solicitation of clients.

In its opinion the Court responded to the argument that advertising would have an adverse effect upon professionalism:

> It is claimed that price advertising will bring about commercialization, which will undermine the attorney's sense of dignity and self-worth. The hustle of the marketplace will adversely affect the profession's service orientation, and irreparably damage the delicate balance between the lawyer's need to earn and his obligation selflessly to serve.
>   . . .
> We recognize, of course, and commend the spirit of public service with which the profession of law is practiced and to which it is dedicated. The present Members of this Court, licensed attorneys all, could not feel otherwise. And we would have reason to pause if we felt that our decision today would undercut that spirit. But we find the postulated connection between advertising and the erosion of true professionalism to be severely strained. At its core, the argument presumes that attorneys must conceal from themselves and from their clients the real-life fact that lawyers earn their livelihood at the bar. We suspect that few attorneys engage in such self-deception. And rare is the client, moreover, even one of the modest means, who enlists the aid of an attorney with the expectation that his services will be rendered free of charge.[34]

The Court noted certain positive consequences of advertising. It provides information that helps the consumer of legal services to arrive at an informed decision in the choice of an attorney. Advertising helps the new members of the profession and those with limited contacts in the community to penetrate the market for legal services. In addition, advertising should increase competition among lawyers, and thereby cause legal services to be available at lower cost. These are the principal professional and social considerations regularly offered in justification of advertising.

In 1985 the Supreme Court ruled that lawyer advertising of a more aggressive nature was constitutionally protected.[35] In that case the lawyer published an ad in newspapers expressing his interest in representing women who had suffered injuries resulting from the use of the contraceptive known as the Dalkon Shield Intrauterine Device. The ad consisted of a drawing of the device, accompanied by the question: "Did You Use This IUD?" It also contained the following information:

> The Dalkon Shield Interuterine [*sic*] Device is alleged to have caused serious pelvic infections resulting in hospitalizations, tubal damage, infertility, and hysterectomies. It is also alleged to have caused unplanned pregnancies ending in abortions, miscarriages, septic abortions, tubal or ectopic pregnancies, and full-term deliveries. If you or a friend have had a similar experience do not assume it is too late to take legal action against the Shield's manufacturer. Our law firm is presently representing women on such cases. The cases are handled on a contingent fee basis of the amount recovered. If there is no recovery, no legal fees are owed by our clients.

The Ohio Supreme Court had issued a public reprimand of the attorney on the grounds that the ad violated several professional rules, one of which required that advertisements "be presented in a dignified manner without the use of drawings, illustrations" and another which prohibited accepting employment resulting from unsolicited legal advice.

The U.S. Supreme Court stated that the information and advice concerning the contraceptive device was not false or deceptive. The Court also dismissed the "dignity" question:

> There is, of course, no suggestion that the illustration actually used by appellant was undignified; thus, it is difficult to see how the application of the rule to appellant in this case directly advances the State's interest in preserving the dignity of attorneys. More fundamentally, although the State undoubtedly has a substantial interest in ensuring that its attorneys behave with dignity and decorum in the courtroom, we are unsure that the State's desire that attorneys maintain their dignity in their communications with the public is an interest substantial enough to justify the abridgment of their First Amendment rights.[36]

The significance of this decision is that accurate information and advice in ads directed at individuals who have experienced specified harm are constitutionally protected. In addition, the Court indicated that dignity probably is not a justification for restraints upon lawyer advertising.

In 1988 the Supreme Court ruled that a truthful and nondeceptive letter sent by a lawyer to a potential client known to have a particular legal problem is protected under the First Amendment.[37] The letter that was the subject of the litigation read as follows:

It has come to my attention that your home is being foreclosed on. If this is true, you may be about to lose your home. Federal law may allow you to keep your home by ORDERING your creditor [*sic*] to STOP and give you more time to pay them.

You may call my office anytime from 8:30 A.M. to 5:00 P.M. for FREE information on how you can keep your home.

Call NOW, don't wait. It may surprise you what I may be able to do for you. Just call and tell me that you got this letter. Remember it is FREE, there is NO charge for calling.

The Kentucky professional rules in question prohibited in-person solicitation and solicitation by letter to persons known to be in need of legal services in a particular matter.

In-person solicitation has generally been prohibited by professional rules. In 1978 the Supreme Court upheld the constitutionality of the prohibition against such solicitation when the lawyer's purpose is pecuniary gain.[38] Although in-person solicitation involves speech, the danger of overreaching and undue influence by the lawyer upon the potential client in that circumstance justifies the restriction. In its 1988 decision the Supreme Court distinguished solicitation by mail from in-person solicitation on the ground that the dangers of overreaching and undue influence are not present in the former circumstance—the recipient can simply drop the letter in the wastebasket. As a result of this decision, individuals who receive speeding tickets or who are injured in accidents now regularly receive a number of letters from lawyers soliciting their business.

Justice O'Connor wrote a powerful dissenting opinion in the "solicitation by mail" case, in which Chief Justice Rehnquist and Justice Scalia joined. The salient portions of that dissent are as follows:

It is worth recalling why lawyers are regulated at all, or to a greater degree than most other occupations. . . . Operating a legal system that is both reasonably efficient and tolerably fair cannot be accomplished, at least under modern social conditions, without a trained and specialized body of experts. This training is one element of what we mean when we refer to the law as a "learned profession." Such knowledge by its nature cannot be made generally available, and it therefore confers the power and the temptation to manipulate the system of justice for one's own ends. Such manipulation can occur in at least two obvious ways. One results from overly zealous representation of the client's interests; abuse of the discovery process is one example whose causes and effects (if not its cure) is apparent. The second, and for present purposes the more relevant, problem is abuse of the client for the lawyer's benefit.

. . .

Restrictions on advertising and solicitation . . . act as a concrete, day-to-day reminder to the practicing attorney of why it is improper for any member of this profession to regard it as a trade or occupation like any other.

. . .

Whatever may be the exactly appropriate scope of these restrictions at a given time and place, this Court's recent decisions reflect a myopic belief that "consumers," and thus our Nation, will benefit from a constitutional theory that refuses to recognize either the essence of professionalism or its fragile and necessary foundations.[39]

The cases discussed above constitutionally protect advertising and targeted mail solicitation, regardless of their tastelessness or lack of dignity, as long as the information and advice contained therein are not false or misleading. In 1995 the Supreme Court, in a five-to-four decision, changed direction.[40] The Florida Bar had adopted a rule prohibiting targeted mail solicitation by lawyers of accident or disaster victims and their families for thirty days following the accident or disaster. The Supreme Court ruled that this restriction was constitutionally permissible because of the substantial state interests served by the restriction. One interest is the protection of the privacy and tranquillity of victims and their families from the offense and intrusion of such commercial solicitation. The other interest is the prevention of the erosion of confidence in the legal profession that results from such insensitive behavior. The opinion of the majority was written, not surprisingly, by Justice O'Connor.

In one sense the 1995 decision is a very limited one; it permits a restriction of short duration upon solicitation of a special class of potential clients. But in another sense the decision has broad implications because for the first time the court held that the protection of the reputation of the profession was a state interest that justified a restriction upon the commercial speech of lawyers. This may encourage states to adopt restrictions on advertising that is considered to be in poor taste and to reflect adversely upon the reputation of the bar. Certainly some television advertising by lawyers is considered by many to be in that category. How far the rationale of this decision extends will be determined by future litigation challenging any future restrictions.

There is a form of publicity that differs from the advertising and targeted mail solicitation that have been the subject of the cases discussed. It is referred to as "marketing." Law firms that represent large corporations do not advertise in newspapers or on television. To attract new business, they distribute to corporate officers sophisticated brochures describing the credentials of their lawyers and the nature of the work they do. These firms also conduct seminars in areas of the law of interest to prospective corporate clients and distribute newsletters on recent legal developments. Large corporate law firms often have public relations and marketing staffs. The aggressive pursuit of business is occurring at all levels.

What are the pros and cons of all these practices, which may be generically referred to as advertising? One argument for the practice is that it educates the consumer of legal services. The consumer learns who does the kind of legal work the consumer has a need for, what the lawyer's background and qualifications are, and sometimes what the fee is or how it is determined. For example, an ad for a personal injury lawyer may inform the consumer that there is a fee only if the client receives payment for his injury by settlement or court judgment. In addition, the ad may explain that the consumer who has suffered a certain type of injury may have a legal claim for damages.

Another argument for advertising is that it has the effect of increasing competition among lawyers by making known their availability, thereby driving down the price for legal services. This assertion is conjectural, but there is some support for it.[41] Another positive argument is that it provides access to the market for legal services to the newcomer to the profession or to a geographical area, as well as to the person who lacks social connections. It should be noted that television advertising is extremely expensive and therefore may serve to entrench the prosperous established lawyer and exclude the newcomer.

It is interesting that support for advertising comes from both the social left and the libertarian right. The left sees it as providing opportunity for the professional underdog, and the libertarian right sees it as a function of the free market for legal services, which should result in a better product being available at a lower price.

Those who oppose advertising contend that it is often undignified and reflects poorly upon the profession. In addition, there are substantive objections that the aggressive pursuit of business may affect the lawyer's relationship to the client and the advice that is given. Let us assume, as is often the case, that the client has an objective for which the legal consequences are ambiguous—that is, there is an argument that can be made for its legality and an argument against it. The lawyer should inform the client of these conflicting considerations and offer her judgment as to the weight to be given to each. Clients, however, prefer good news to bad news. The aggressive pursuit of the client may affect the lawyer's objectivity and make it more likely that she will emphasize what the client wants to hear. This is not something that lends itself to empirical confirmation, but it is inferentially plausible and maybe convincing.

Closely related is the objection that the aggressive pursuit of business makes it unlikely the lawyer will perform in accordance with the "independent lawyer" model. The independent lawyer not only provides objective advice with respect to legality, but also counsels the client concerning the long-term impact of proposed action on the client's interests and concerning the social and moral consequences of proposed action. The lawyer thereby serves as a constraining influence upon the client's behavior. It is unlikely that the lawyer who has aggressively pursued the client would be inclined to act as a constraining influence upon the client whose objective is legal but socially damaging. There is a judgmental quality to the role of the independent lawyer that does not mesh with the active solicitation of business.

Finally, there is the objection so forcefully presented by Justice O'Connor in her dissent in the targeted mail solicitation case. The layperson is at the mercy of the lawyer because of the latter's "expertise which is both esoteric and powerful." The professional rules prohibit the lawyer from using her power to exploit the client for the lawyer's benefit. Economic self-interest, however, is a "relentless natural force," and the spirit of advertising feeds that drive. Restrictions upon advertising are required to preserve the "fragile and necessary foundations" of professionalism.[42]

COMMERCIALISM

Lawyers earn their living by providing a service involving expenses that must be paid. In this respect it is a business. It differs, however, from the commercial enterprise because of the constraints imposed upon the lawyer. The lawyer is a fiduciary for the client; she must serve the client's interests and not her own. The lawyer must provide her professional service at the lowest cost consistent with effective representation. The traditional ideology of the profession defines it as a public service by which the lawyer earns her living. Unlike private enterprise generally, it is not a profit-maximizing endeavor.

In recent years there has been a change in the ethos of the profession. The business aspect is being emphasized as never before.[43] The late Justice Potter Stewart of the U.S. Supreme Court captured this spirit:

> It goes without saying, of course, that every lawyer has a duty to keep the confidences of his client, that every lawyer in whom is confided a trust must conduct himself as a trustee, that every lawyer should keep his word and deal honorably in all his associations. And it certainly is the duty of every lawyer, and of every association of lawyers, to denounce and to eliminate from our midst those who have betrayed our profession for their own ugly or dishonest purposes.
>
> But beyond these and a few other self-evident precepts of decency and common sense, a good case can be made, I think, for the proposition that the ethics of the business lawyer are indeed, and perhaps should be, no more than the morals of the market place. The first rule for a business lawyer is to provide his total ability and effort to his client. But is this an ethical standard, or not more than a response to the economic forces of the market place? After all, the first rule in any occupation is to be competent. The business lawyer is in the business of providing legal advice for a businessman. If he performs that job with diligence, conscientiousness, and knowledgeable ability, his client will reap the benefits and will reward him accordingly. If not, unless he is particularly lucky or married to the boss' daughter, the lawyer will find his client less than eager to retain indefinitely a professional adviser who habitually directs him down the wrong path.

> In short, it can fairly be argued that many aspects of what we call "ethics" are not really ethics at all, but are merely corollaries of the axiom of the better mousetrap, an axiom that is itself derived from enlightened self-interest.[44]

In affording constitutional protection to lawyer advertising, the Supreme Court acknowledged that the practice of law is a business. The aggressive pursuit of business—a defining characteristic of the free market—is now routine for lawyers at all levels of practice. Most of the television advertising by lawyers is directed at individuals who have suffered physical injuries and may have claims for damages. This form of advertising is very expensive and is obviously productive for the lawyers engaged in it. It usually does not inform or educate the consumer in any fashion, but merely publicizes the identity of the lawyer. The number of personal injury victims is fixed, and television advertising serves to direct them to those lawyers who use it. This forces other personal injury lawyers to advertise in order to maintain their share of the market. The advertising industry prospers, but no social purpose is served. Indeed, because of its cost, the practice tends to establish a barrier to entry by young lawyers who do not have the capital required to use the medium.

The large corporate firm tailors its aggressive pursuit of business to its clients. There is no need to advertise on television because potential clients are readily identifiable. Brochures describing the firm and its capabilities, seminars on corporate legal matters, newsletters on legal developments, and outings at country clubs are the means appropriate to the client.

There is no doubt that the profession has become increasingly money-conscious. This is further evidenced by the popularity of continuing legal education courses on profitability and the appearance in the legal press of rankings of firms' incomes, which, of course, have been voluntarily disclosed. One commentator has summed up the situation:

> Lawyers historically have commanded high fees and made money in the practice of law. What is new in the last decade, however, is published data about lawyers' income; analyses of economic successes and failures; the creation of conferences and educational programs devoted to increasing profitability and the economic success of law practice; and the emergence of a new industry of law-practice consultants and nonlawyer managers who attend to the profitability of the practice, the attraction of talent, and marketing and public relations. The legal profession, in the decade of the 1980s and 1990s, has become extraordinarily self-conscious about making money. The tools of the new legal journalism hone this self-consciousness to a sharp comparative and competitive edge.[45]

Associates (lawyer-employees) are a substantial source of income for the partners of large law firms. The billing of clients is based, in large part, on the hours expended by the lawyers in the firm. A significant portion of the rate charged for an associate's time constitutes profit for the partners. Associates are told that they are expected to bill a certain number of hours annually, such as 2,000, and in some firms, more than that. Two thousand billed hours amounts to much more than forty hours of work a week, given vacations, holidays, medical and other absences, and time that is not billable, such as time spent on administrative matters and keeping current in one's area of practice. In addition, there are the inevitable hours that are not efficiently used. It is made clear that an associate's prospects in the firm are dependent upon the revenues she produces. A partner's performance is measured to a considerable extent by the degree to which he "leverages" associates—that is, produces revenue from associates' billed time. Under these circumstances, it is likely that the associate is going to produce the expected billed hours. Billing based on time has been analogized to cost-plus contracting practices—it compensates inefficiency and contains substantial moral risk.[46]

Current practice contrasts sharply with practices forty years ago when the author worked for a large law firm. The associate kept a daily time-sheet and the partners made a profit on his work. The associate was not advised, however, that he was expected to bill a specified number of hours each year. The associate was expected to do the work assigned to him in a timely fashion. Sometimes the work assigned required staying in the office in the evening or going to work on Saturday, but usually it was doable during normal working hours. The billing was based on a mix of considerations including time spent, the size and importance of the matter, and the professional skill required to do the job. The time-sheet was important for cost-management and billing, and certainly the associate's work produced profits for the partners. The associate was valued, however, for the quality of his work. Unquestionably he was a form of revenue-producing capital as well, but he was not made to believe that was his primary function.[47]

It is a professional sin for the lawyer to use her knowledge and power to exploit the client for the lawyer's personal gain. Commercialism is not necessarily in conflict with the lawyer's fiduciary obligation to the client, but the former may place a strain on the latter. Justice Sandra Day O'Connor has spoken of the tension between the force of economic self-interest and professional duty.

> Like physicians, lawyers are subjected to heightened ethical demands on their conduct towards those they serve. These demands are needed because market forces, and the ordinary legal prohibitions against force and fraud, are simply insufficient to protect the consumers of their necessary services from the peculiar power of the specialized knowledge that these professionals possess.
>
> Imbuing the legal profession with the necessary ethical standards is a task that involves a constant struggle with the relentless natural force of economic self-interest.[48]

The evidence that in recent years there is more exploitation of clients for personal gain than in the past is anecdotal, but the impression is widespread. Bringing a lawsuit is much more profitable for the lawyer than early settlement. For responsible lawyers, bringing suit is a last resort, not only because of the expense to the client, but also because of the emotional cost of the conflict and the destructive effect upon the relationship of the parties. Many lawyers today do not seem to have an aversion to this civilized form of battle.[49]

After suit is brought and before the trial begins, the process of pre-trial discovery of evidence—consisting of requests for information and documents and the taking of the testimony (depositions) of potential witnesses—is frequently protracted, burdensome to the parties, and expensive. The process of discovery often leads to settlement. If it does not, the trial follows. Either way, there is a lot of money in it for the lawyers.

There is the controversial issue of the lawyer's contingent fee agreement with the client, which provides that if the client settles or wins the suit, the lawyer receives a fee in the amount of, let us say, one-third of what the client recovers, and if the client loses the suit the lawyer receives no fee. Sometimes the percentage is higher. Viewed in isolation, a fee of one-third of what the client receives is very high, but it is deemed to be justified to compensate for the risk of receiving no fee. The lawyer who handles ten cases that could go either way and recovers nothing in five of them, is, in effect, being compensated at the rate of one-half of 33 percent in those cases he wins. This may result in compensation that is high, but not outrageously so. The contingent fee is permitted by the professional rules except in the representation of parties to a divorce proceeding or of criminal defendants.[50] It is used primarily, but not exclusively, in personal injury claims.

The contingent fee places temptation in the lawyer's path. He has a direct personal interest in how the matter is resolved. If the other side offers to settle for substantially less than the lawyer is asking for his client, the lawyer's fee is lower if the settlement offer is accepted than it would be if he sued for his client and recovered what he is asking. If, however, the settlement offer is accepted, the lawyer is assured a fee, which is not the case if the matter goes to trial. The decision as to settlement or trial is the client's to make,[51] but the lawyer's advice is influential. The lawyer is professionally obligated to consider only the interests of the client, of course, but the lawyer's personal interest may conflict with that of the client. The client may be risk-averse, but the lawyer may be personally inclined to a high-risk, high-return strategy, or vice-versa. The lawyer's personal interest also may become a factor if the offer of settlement has been made after the lawyer has devoted a great deal of time to the case; the lawyer may consider the fee that he would receive if the settlement is accepted to be inadequate compensation for his time and would want to go for the risk of higher compensation that may result from a trial.

The profession is very much aware of the moral risks in the contingent fee arrangement. Indeed, the professional rules forbid the lawyer from having a "proprietary" interest in a lawsuit except for the contingent fee.[52] The justification offered for the contingent fee is that many people of modest means who have been injured or have otherwise been harmed cannot afford to hire a lawyer to recover from the wrongdoer except on a contingent fee basis. There is much to be said for this, but the contingent fee is also available to those who *can* afford to hire a lawyer on a conventional fee basis in the personal injury case. The contingent fee is now sometimes used in connection with representation in business deals that may or may not be consummated.[53] The profession could limit the use to the situations that may justify it, but it has not chosen to do so.

The contingent fee is used for the most part by personal injury lawyers; that is, those who represent plaintiffs who have been injured in automobile or other accidents. These lawyers are often specialists who handle a substantial volume of cases, many of them claims in the range of $10,000 or less. In many of these small cases the liability of the defendant is clear and settlement with the defendant's insurance company is routine and quick. There is no risk of there being no fee for the lawyer. Nevertheless, the lawyer receives his contingent fee of one-third. The lawyer, of course, does not accept cases in which it is clear there is no liability. The cases in which liability is problematic and that involve risk to the lawyer and the expenditure of substantial time may balance off and justify the one-third contingent fee, but there is no justification for such a fee in cases in which liability is clear and negotiation is quick. There is exploitation of the client here, and it is arguably a violation of the professional rule prohibiting "unreasonable fees,"[54] but the practice goes on all the time. Simple cases in which liability is clear should be charged on a time basis.

Does commercialism contribute to the erosion of the lawyer's fiduciary obligation to serve the client's interest exclusively and efficiently? No one knows for sure, but it is plausible, and the impression is widespread that it has.

HARDBALL TACTICS

The lawyer is dedicated exclusively and zealously to the interests of his client. This is premised on the belief that adversarial representation is the best means for achieving just results. As discussed in previous chapters, this may be a faulty premise, but it is a given in our system of law. The tradition in the profession has been, however, that in the course of vigorous advocacy on behalf of clients, lawyers are to conduct themselves civilly and courteously in their dealings with each other. Lawyers have professional duties to each other that are independent of their roles as advocates for their clients. The clients may be enemies, but the lawyers are not. This principle of behavior is not honored as it once was.

In the courtroom lawyers engage in insulting exchanges and charge each other with improper conduct. Lawyers often time their filing of documents to allow as little time as possible for the opposing lawyer to prepare his response. Lawyers sometimes refuse to agree to requests for extensions of deadlines for tactical advantage. Depositions may be scheduled so as to inconvenience the opposing attorney or witness. Negotiations are frequently threatening and acrimonious. This behavior does harm to the reputation of the lawyers who use such tactics, but for many that is not a deterrent. The impersonal nature of contemporary urban practice probably has something to do with this phenomenon. Cities are larger today, and there are many more lawyers. There is less of this in small communities where lawyers deal with each other regularly and sometimes socially.[55]

Lawyers sometimes ask questions of witnesses that are impermissible in the circumstances, for the purpose of planting an idea in the minds of the jurors. Opposing counsel objects to the question before the witness can respond. The judge sustains the objection and instructs the jury to disregard the implications of the question. A message has been sent and received by the jurors, and the lawyer has accomplished his objective. Another disreputable tactic is to interrupt opposing counsel with groundless objections while he is making his argument to the jury, for the purpose of slowing his "momentum."

Trial lawyers regularly use the media to advance their clients' interests. Under the professional rules lawyers are forbidden to make out-of-court statements that the lawyer knows will have a substantial likelihood of prejudicing a judicial proceeding.[56] Comments on the character or credibility of a party or witness, comments on the guilt or innocence of a defendant, and information that would be inadmissible in the trial all fall into that category.

In the final section of Chapter 3 we discussed the abuses of the pre-trial discovery process. Excessive and manipulative discovery practices can be very expensive and burdensome. These tactics can be a weapon to discourage litigation or to induce settlement on terms that are less favorable to the deserving party than they should be. They constitute a particularly potent weapon when used by a party with large resources against a party with limited resources. Although such practices are used for the purpose of harassment, they are often within the professional rules because there is a basis for the conduct, however marginal, that is substantively relevant to the litigation. Abusive discovery practices constitute the most significant professional problem in litigation today. The mandatory disclosure reform discussed at the end of Chapter 3 was intended to deal with it, but the effectiveness of the reform remains to be seen.

It is not suggested that "hardball" tactics are new to the profession. What is disturbing is that they are now so widely accepted and practiced.

Indeed, it is often contended that they are required as zealous advocacy on behalf of the client. The constraints of civility, courtesy, and decency have been forgotten in the battle on behalf of the client.[57]

CONCLUSION

Lawyers perform a vast array of tasks that are essential to an orderly, productive, and free society. They represent parties in their disputes with one another and with the state. They design regimes for the production of wealth and the arrangements for its transfer. They guide citizens through the thicket of taxation and governmental regulation. It seems that the practice of law should have the respect of the public, but in fact it is not held in high regard. The profession has itself to blame. The disrepute has to do with how lawyers go about their tasks.

The root of the problem is in a particular interpretation of the lawyer's duty to his client and the behavioral excesses that derive from that interpretation. If the perceived duty is to obtain whatever the lawyer can for his client, without regard to the legitimate interests of or the harm to others, it follows that all means short of lies, fraud, and crime are appropriate in pursuit of the goal. This is the "hired gun" or "sporting" theory of representation, a contest with its own rules devoid of moral meaning. Although this perception of the lawyer's duty is as old as the profession, it seems that the competitiveness and acquisitiveness of contemporary practice have caused lawyers to embrace this standard of behavior to a greater degree than in the past.

How much better it would be for society, the profession, and lawyers personally if the duty owed to the client was limited to what the client was entitled to under the law applicable to the representation. This may be described as the "justice" theory of representation. If this were the professional standard required of lawyers, there would be no reason, for the most part, to use injurious tactics. It is not suggested that the adversarial method be abandoned, but rather that it be limited to honest differences concerning facts and law. Many lawyers practice this way today, as in the past.

The physician's purpose is to provide the patient the benefit of medical knowledge. The lawyer's purpose should be to provide the client the benefit of the law, no more and no less. That is public service, the essence of professionalism.

Notes

1. Stephen L. Pepper, The Lawyer's Amoral Ethical Role: A Defense, A Problem, and Some Possibilities, 1986 *American Bar Foundation Research Journal* 613, 635.

2. Roger C. Cramton, *Professionalism, Legal Services, and Lawyer Competency*, in American Bar Association, Justice for a Generation 144, 149 (1985).

3. See Archibald Cox, *The Condition of Independence for the Legal Profession,* in American Bar Association, The Lawyer's Professional Independence 53 (1984); Robert W. Gordon, The Independence of Lawyers, 68 *Boston University Law Review* 1, 33–38 (1988); Anthony T. Kronman, The Lost Lawyer 15 (Belknap, 1993).

4. Model Rule 1.3, Comment.

5. Model Rule 1.16(b)(3).

6. Model Rule 2.1.

7. Cramton, *supra* note 2, at 149; Gordon, *supra* note 3, at 24; Richard L. Abel, American Lawyers 247 (Oxford, 1989); Mary Ann Glendon, A Nation Under Lawyers 33–39 (Farrar, Straus and Giroux, 1994); Sol M. Linowitz, The Betrayed Profession 10, 18, 19 (Scribner's, 1994).

8. George Sharswood, *Professional Ethics,* in Reports of the American Bar Association, Volume 32, page 83 (T. and J. W. Johnson, 1907).

9. *Id.* at 96.

10. David Hoffman, A Course of Legal Study 754 (Arno, 1972).

11. 2 Herndon's Lincoln 345n. (W. Herndon and J. Weik ed., Herndon's Lincoln Publishing Co., 1888).

12. Louis D. Brandeis, Business: A Profession 321 (Small, Maynard, 1914).

13. Woodrow Wilson, *The Lawyer and the Community,* in 21 The Papers of Woodrow Wilson 66, 69 (A. Link ed., Princeton, 1976).

14. Cox, *supra* note 3, at 59, 61.

15. Roger C. Cramton, *The Lawyer's Professional Independence: Memories, Aspirations, and Realities,* in American Bar Association, The Lawyer's Professional Independence 52 (1985).

16. Mark Galanter and Thomas Palay, Tournament of Lawyers 33, 34 (Chicago, 1991); Kronman, *supra* note 3, at 277; Glendon, *supra* note 7, at 35–37; Gordon, *supra* note 3, at 56.

17. Galanter and Palay, *supra* note 16, at 37–52; Kronman, *supra* note 3, at 284; Glendon, *supra* note 7, at 25; Linowitz, *supra* note 7, at 88, 187; Michael H. Trotter, Profit and the Practice of Law 44, 94 (Georgia, 1997).

18. Abram Chayes and Antonia H. Chayes, Corporate Counsel and the Elite Law Firm, 37 *Stanford Law Review* 277, 290, 293 (1985); Ronald J. Gilson and Robert H. Mnookin, Sharing Among the Human Capitalists: An Economic Inquiry into the Corporate Law Firm and How Partners Split Profits, 37 *Stanford Law Review* 313, 382 (1985); Abel, *supra* note 7, at 171; Kronman, *supra* note 3, at 308–310; Linowitz, *supra* note 7, at 83–84, 88.

19. Chayes and Chayes, *supra* note 18, at 204; Kronman, *supra* note 3, at 276, 285; Galanter and Palay, *supra* note 16, at 114; Linowitz, *supra* note 7, at 39; Michael J. Kelly, Lives of Lawyers: Journeys in the Organization of Practice 175 (Michigan, 1994).

20. Kronman, *supra* note 3, at 276; Galanter and Palay, *supra* note 16, at 50; Linowitz, *supra* note 7, at 45; Kelley, *supra* note 19, at 177.

21. American Bar Association, Lawyer Advertising at the Crossroads 55 (1995); Galanter and Palay, *supra* note 16, at 53; Abel, *supra* note 7, at 121.

22. Gordon, *supra* note 3, at 54; Robert A. Kagan and Robert E. Rosen, On the Social Significance of Large Firm Practice, 37 *Stanford Law Review* 399, 427–430, 439–443 (1985); Robert L. Nelson, Partners with Power: The Social Transforma-

tion of the Large Law Firm 263, 282 (California, 1988); Glendon, *supra* note 7, at 33–37; Kronman, *supra* note 3, at 286–288.

23. Chayes and Chayes, *supra* note 18, at 298; Linowitz, *supra* note 7, at 83–84; Kronman, *supra* note 3, at 379. For a contrary view, see Gordon, *supra* note 3, at 66; Kelly, *supra* note 19, at 91.

24. Galanter and Palay, *supra* note 16, at 23–30; Glendon, *supra* note 7, at 21–22; Kronman *supra* note 3, at 277.

25. Galanter and Palay, *supra* note 16, at 54; Kronman, *supra* note 3, at 277–279.

26. Roscoe Pound, The Lawyer from Antiquity to Modern Times 5 (West, 1953).

27. American Bar Association, Lawyer Advertising at the Crossroads 30–31 (1955). For a survey of the law of advertising by lawyers, see Louise L. Hill, Lawyer Advertising (Quorum, 1993).

28. American Bar Association, Lawyer Advertising at the Crossroads 33 (1995); Jerold S. Auerbach, Unequal Justice 40–43 (Oxford, 1976).

29. Charles W. Wolfram, Modern Legal Ethics 55–56 (West, 1986).

30. *Id.* at 56.

31. Virginia State Board of Pharmacy v. Virginia Citizens Consumer Council, 425 U.S. 748 (1976).

32. 433 U.S. 350 (1977).

33. *Id.* at 384.

34. *Id.* at 368–369.

35. Zauderer v. Office of Disciplinary Counsel, 471 U.S. 626 (1985).

36. *Id.* at 647–648.

37. Shapero v. Kentucky Bar Association, 486 U.S. 466 (1988).

38. Ohralik v. Ohio State Bar Association, 436 U.S. 447 (1978). In-person solicitation for the purpose of furthering some social or political objective, and not primarily for pecuniary gain, is protected under the First Amendment, so long as there is no overreaching or misrepresentation. In Re Primus, 436 U.S. 412 (1978).

39. Shapero v. Kentucky Bar Association, 486 U.S. 466, 489–490 (1988).

40. Florida Bar v. Went For It, Inc., 115 S.C. 237 (1995).

41. There is support for the position that there is economic advantage to the consumer as a consequence of lawyer advertising. See Geoffrey C. Hazard, Russell G. Pearce, and Jeffrey W. Stempel, Why Lawyers Should Be Allowed to Advertise: A Market Analysis of Legal Services, 58 *New York University Law Review* 1084 (1983); Terry Calvani, James Langenfeld, and Gordon Shuford, Attorney Advertising and Competition at the Bar, 41 *Vanderbilt Law Review* 761 (1988); American Bar Association, Lawyer Advertising at the Crossroads 127–134 (1995).

42. Shapero v. Kentucky Bar Association, 486 U.S. 466, 489–90 (1988).

43. Kronman, *supra* note 3, at 296–297, 370; Kelly, *supra* note 19, at 170; Galanter and Palay, *supra* note 16, at 52.

44. Potter Stewart, Professional Ethics for the Business Lawyer: The Morals of the Market Place, 31 *The Business Lawyer* 463 (1975).

45. Kelly, *supra* note 19 at 170. See Kronman, *supra* note 3, at 299; Trotter, *supra* note 17, at 182.

46. Kronman, *supra* note 3, at 302; Linowitz, *supra* note 7, at 107–108; Nelson, *supra* note 22, at 77; Kelly, *supra* note 19, at 31; Eve Spangler, Lawyers for Hire 55

(Yale, 1986); William Ross, The Ethics of Hourly Billing by Attorneys, 44 *Rutgers Law Review* 1 (1991).

47. Glendon, *supra* note 7, at 29.

48. Shapero v. Kentucky Bar Association, 486 U.S. 466, 490 (1988).

49. See Chayes and Chayes, *supra* note 18, at 296–297; Glendon, *supra* note 7, at 55–59; Trotter, *supra* note 17, at 115.

50. Model Rule 1.5(d). The prohibition upon the contingent fee in marital matters seems to be based on the notion that monetary gain should not influence the lawyer's behavior in the resolution of marital conflict and in the determination of the amount of alimony, child support, and property settlement. The prohibition upon the contingent fee in the criminal defense seems to be based on the notion that the lawyer would be tempted to conduct himself dishonorably in order to assure a fee. It seems that these arguments have validity for all areas of legal representation.

51. Model Rule 1.2(a).

52. Model Rule 1.8(j).

53. Glendon, *supra* note 7, at 54; Linowitz, *supra* note 7, at 89, 105–106.

54. Model Rule 1.5(a). There are some judicial decisions and opinions of ethics committees of state bars to the effect that contingent fees in riskless cases are unethical. However, enforcement is almost nonexistent because of the practical problems of case-by-case determination by the courts or disciplinary bodies that there is no risk. See Lester Brickman, Michael Horowitz, and Jeffrey O'Connell, Rethinking Contingency Fees (Manhattan Institute, 1994); Derek Bok, The Cost of Talent 139–144 (Free Press, 1993).

55. Donald D. Landon, Country Lawyers 140–146 (Praeger, 1990).

56. Model Rule 3.6.

57. See Kathleen P. Browe, A Critique of the Civility Movement: Why Rambo Will Not Go Away, 77 *Marquette Law Review* 751 (1994); Robert N. Sayler, Rambo Litigation—Why Hardball Tactics Don't Work, 74 *American Bar Association Journal,* March 1988, at page 79; Peter M. Brown, Narcissism, Manners, and Morals: Can Grace and Collegiality Be Salvaged?, 13 *Litigation* 2, Winter 1987, at page 17; Trotter, *supra* note 17, at 128.

Appendix:
Excerpts from Professional Rules

The professional rules set forth below are those referred to in the text. The American Bar Association (ABA) promulgated the Model Rules of Professional Conduct in 1983. The ABA is a private organization that has no legal authority over the profession. The ABA Model Rules constitute a recommendation to the states; a substantial majority of the states have adopted the Model Rules, invariably with certain changes. The states that have not adopted the Model Rules have, for the most part, the professional rules promulgated by the ABA in 1969, which the ABA replaced in 1983. There are certain substantial differences between the two sets of rules, but for the most part the differences are in style and form.

The 1983 ABA Model Rules contain extensive explanatory Comments to the Rules. The ABA has copyrighted the Model Rules and the Comments. For reasons best known to the ABA, it would not grant permission to reproduce specific Rules in this appendix without the inclusion in full of the Comments to those Rules as well. The inclusion of the Comments would treble the length of the appendix. For the most part, the Comments are not pertinent to the purpose of this book and would be a burdensome distraction for the lay reader. This appendix is intended for the lay reader; the lawyer has the Rules and Comments available to him.

In order to overcome the obstacle created by the ABA, this appendix contains a number of the professional rules adopted by the state of Missouri that are identical in their language and numbering to the ABA Rules; Missouri Rule 3.6, which is similar to its ABA counterpart; and Rules 7.1, 7.2(a), and 7.3(a) of the state of South Carolina, which are identical in their language and numbering to their ABA counterparts. Several brief portions of pertinent Comments that are identical to their ABA counterparts are also included. So the author has achieved indirectly that which the ABA denied directly.

RULE 1.2:
SCOPE OF REPRESENTATION (MISSOURI)

...

(d) A lawyer shall not counsel a client to engage, or assist a client, in conduct that the lawyer knows is criminal or fraudulent, but a lawyer may discuss the legal consequences of any proposed course of conduct with a client and may counsel or assist a client to make a good faith effort to determine the validity, scope, meaning or application of the law.

. . .

RULE 1.3: DILIGENCE (MISSOURI)

A lawyer shall act with reasonable diligence and promptness in representing a client.

Comment

A lawyer should pursue a matter on behalf of a client despite opposition, obstruction or personal inconvenience to the lawyer, and may take whatever lawful and ethical measures are required to vindicate a client's cause or endeavor. A lawyer should act with commitment and dedication to the interests of the client and with zeal in advocacy upon the client's behalf. However, a lawyer is not bound to press for every advantage that might be realized for a client. A lawyer has professional discretion in determining the means by which a matter should be pursued.

. . .

RULE 1.5: FEES (MISSOURI)

. . .

(c) A fee may be contingent on the outcome of the matter for which the service is rendered, except in a matter in which a contingent fee is prohibited by paragraph (d) or other law. A contingent fee agreement shall be in writing and shall state the method by which the fee is to be determined, including the percentage or percentages that shall accrue to the lawyer in the event of settlement, trial or appeal, litigation and other expenses to be deducted from the recovery, and whether such expenses are to be deducted before or after the contingent fee is calculated. . . .

(d) A lawyer shall not enter into an arrangement for, charge, or collect:

(1) any fee in a domestic relations matter, the payment or amount of which is contingent upon the securing of a divorce or upon the amount of alimony or support, or property settlement in lieu thereof; or

(2) a contingent fee for representing a defendant in a criminal case.

. . .

RULE 1.6: CONFIDENTIALITY OF INFORMATION (MISSOURI)

(a) A lawyer shall not reveal information relating to representation of a client unless the client consents after consultation, except for disclosures that are impliedly authorized in order to carry out the representation, and except as stated in paragraph (b).

(b) A lawyer may reveal such information to the extent the lawyer reasonably believes necessary:

(1) to prevent the client from committing a criminal act that the lawyer believes is likely to result in imminent death or substantial bodily harm; or

(2) to establish a claim or defense on behalf of the lawyer in a controversy between the lawyer and the client, to establish a defense to a criminal charge or civil claim against the lawyer based upon conduct in which the client was involved, or to respond to allegations in any proceeding concerning the lawyer's representation of the client.

[Unlike 1.6(b)(1) above, a majority of states permit the lawyer to reveal the client's intention to commit any type of crime.]

RULE 1.8: CONFLICT OF INTEREST: PROHIBITED TRANSACTIONS (MISSOURI)

. . .

(j) A lawyer shall not acquire a proprietary interest in the cause of action or subject matter of litigation the lawyer is conducting for a client, except that the lawyer may:

(1) acquire a lien granted by law to secure the lawyer's fee or expenses; and

(2) contract with a client for a reasonable contingent fee in a civil case.

RULE 1.16: DECLINING OR TERMINATING REPRESENTATION (MISSOURI)

. . .

(b) Except at stated in paragraph c, a lawyer may withdraw from representing a client if withdrawal can be accomplished without material adverse effect on the interests of the client, or if:

(1) the client persists in a course of action involving the lawyer's services that the lawyer reasonably believes is criminal or fraudulent;

(2) the client has used the lawyer's services to perpetrate a crime or fraud;

(3) a client insists upon pursuing an objective that the lawyer considers repugnant or imprudent;

. . .

RULE 2.1: ADVISOR (MISSOURI)

In representing a client, a lawyer shall exercise independent professional judgment and render candid advice. In rendering advice, a lawyer may refer not only to law but to other considerations such as moral, economic, social and political factors, that may be relevant to the client's situation.

RULE 3.1: MERITORIOUS CLAIMS AND CONTENTIONS (MISSOURI)

A lawyer shall not bring or defend a proceeding, or assert or controvert an issue therein, unless there is a basis for doing so that is not frivolous, which includes a good faith argument for an extension, modification or reversal of existing law. . . .

Comment

The filing of an action or defense or similar action taken for a client is not frivolous merely because the facts have not first been fully substantiated or because the lawyer expects to develop vital evidence only by discovery. Such action is not frivolous even though the lawyer believes that the client's position ultimately will not prevail.

RULE 3.2: EXPEDITING LITIGATION (MISSOURI)

A lawyer shall make reasonable efforts to expedite litigation consistent with the interests of the client.

Comment

Dilatory practices bring the administration of justice into disrepute. Delay should not be indulged merely for the convenience of the advocates, or for the purpose of frustrating an opposing party's attempt to obtain rightful redress or repose. . . . The question is whether a competent lawyer acting in good faith would regard the course of action as having some substantial purpose other than delay. . . .

RULE 3.3: CANDOR TOWARD THE TRIBUNAL (MISSOURI)

(a) A lawyer shall not knowingly:
(1) make a false statement of material fact or law to a tribunal;
(2) fail to disclose a material fact to a tribunal when disclosure is necessary to avoid assisting a criminal or fraudulent act by the client;
(3) fail to disclose to the tribunal legal authority in the controlling jurisdiction known to the lawyer to be directly adverse to the position of the client and not disclosed by opposing counsel; or
(4) offer evidence that the lawyer knows to be false. If a lawyer has offered material evidence and comes to know of its falsity, the lawyer shall take reasonable remedial measures.
(b) The duties stated in paragraph (a) continue to the conclusion of the proceeding, and apply even if compliance requires disclosure of information otherwise protected by rule 1.6.
. . .

RULE 3.4: FAIRNESS TO OPPOSING PARTY AND COUNSEL (MISSOURI)

A lawyer shall not:

(a) unlawfully obstruct another party's access to evidence or unlawfully alter, destroy or conceal a document or other material having potential evidentiary value. A lawyer shall not counsel or assist another person to do any such act;
(b) falsify evidence, counsel or assist a witness to testify falsely, or offer an inducement to a witness that is prohibited by law;
. . .

RULE 3.6: TRIAL PUBLICITY (MISSOURI)

(a) A lawyer shall not make an extrajudicial statement that a reasonable person would expect to be disseminated by means of public communication if the lawyer knows or reasonably should know that it will have a substantial likelihood of materially prejudicing an adjudicative proceeding.
(b) A statement referred to in paragraph (a) ordinarily is likely to have such an effect when it refers to a civil matter triable to a jury, a criminal matter, or any other proceeding that could result in incarceration and the statement relates to:

(1) the character, credibility, reputation or criminal record of a party, suspect in a criminal investigation or witness, or the identity of a witness, or the expected testimony of a party or witness;

. . .

(4) any opinion as to the guilt or innocence of a defendant or suspect in a criminal case or proceeding that could result in incarceration;

. . .

RULE 4.1: TRUTHFULNESS IN STATEMENTS TO OTHERS (MISSOURI)

In the course of representing a client a lawyer shall not knowingly:

(a)   make a false statement of material fact or law to a third person.

. . .

Comment

. . .

This Rule refers to statements of fact. Whether a particular statement should be regarded as one of fact can depend on the circumstances. Under generally accepted conventions in negotiation, certain types of statements ordinarily are not taken as statements of material fact. Estimates of price or value placed on the subject of a transaction and a party's intentions as to an acceptable settlement of a claim are in this category. . . .

. . .

RULE 4.3: DEALING WITH UNREPRESENTED PERSON (MISSOURI)

In dealing on behalf of a client with a person who is not represented by counsel, a lawyer shall not state or imply that the lawyer is disinterested. When the lawyer knows or reasonably should know that the unrepresented person misunderstands the lawyer's role in the matter, the lawyer shall make reasonable efforts to correct the misunderstanding.

Comment

An unrepresented person, particularly one not experienced in dealing with legal matters, might assume that a lawyer is disinterested in loyalties or is a disinterested authority on the law even when the lawyer represents a client. During the course of a lawyer's representation of a client, the lawyer should not give advice to an unrepresented person other than the advice to obtain counsel.

RULE 4.4: RESPECT FOR RIGHTS OF THIRD PERSONS (MISSOURI)

In representing a client, a lawyer shall not use means that have no substantial purpose other than to embarrass, delay, or burden a third person, or use methods of obtaining evidence that violate the legal rights of such a person.

RULE 7.1: COMMUNICATIONS CONCERNING A LAWYER'S SERVICES (SOUTH CAROLINA)

A lawyer shall not make a false or misleading communication about the lawyer or the lawyer's services. A communication is false or misleading if it:

(a) contains a material misrepresentation of fact or law, or omits a fact necessary to make the statement considered as a whole not materially misleading;

(b) is likely to create an unjustified expectation about results the lawyer can achieve, or states or implies that the lawyer can achieve results by means that violate the Rules of Professional Conduct or other law; or

(c) compares the lawyer's services with other lawyers' services, unless the comparison can be factually substantiated.

Comment

This Rule governs all communications about a lawyer's services, including advertising permitted by Rule 7.2. Whatever means are used to make known a lawyer's services, statements about them should be truthful. The prohibition in paragraph (b) of statements that may create "unjustified expectations" would ordinarily preclude advertisements about results obtained on behalf of a client, such as the amount of a damage award or the lawyer's record in obtaining favorable verdicts, and advertisements containing client endorsements. Such information may create the unjustified expectation that similar results can be obtained for others without reference to the specific factual and legal circumstances.

RULE 7.2: ADVERTISING (SOUTH CAROLINA)

(a) Subject to the requirements of Rules 7.1 and 7.3, a lawyer may advertise services through public media, such as a telephone directory, legal directory, newspaper or other periodical, outdoor advertising, radio or television, or through written or recorded communication.

. . .

RULE 7.3: DIRECT CONTACT WITH PROSPECTIVE CLIENTS (SOUTH CAROLINA)

(a) A lawyer shall not by in-person or live telephone contact solicit professional employment from a prospective client with whom the lawyer has no family or prior professional relationship when a significant motive for the lawyer's doing so is the lawyer's pecuniary gain.

. . .

RULE 8.4: MISCONDUCT (MISSOURI)

It is professional misconduct for a lawyer to:

(a) violate or attempt to violate the Rules of Professional Conduct, knowingly assist or induce another to do so, or do so through the acts of another;
(b) commit a criminal act that reflects adversely on the lawyer's honesty, trustworthiness or fitness as a lawyer in other respects;
(c) engage in conduct involving dishonesty, fraud, deceit or misrepresentation;
(d) engage in conduct that is prejudicial to the administration of justice.

. . .

RULE 9.1: DEFINITION OF TERMS (MISSOURI)

"Fraud" or "fraudulent" denotes conduct having a purpose to deceive and not merely negligent misrepresentation or failure to apprise another of relevant information.

"Knowingly," "known," or "knows" denotes actual knowledge of the fact in question. A person's knowledge may be inferred from circumstances.

"Reasonable" or "reasonably" when used in relation to conduct by a lawyer denotes the conduct of a reasonably prudent and competent lawyer.

. . .

Index

Abusive practices, 104
Adversary system, 52, 55
Advertising by lawyers
  dignity, 95, 97
  1800s, 92–93
  First Amendment, 94
  justifications, 94, 97–98
  marketing compared, 97, 100
  objections, 96, 98
  professionalism, 94, 99
  prohibitions upon, 93
  Supreme Court decisions,
    94–97
  targeted mailing, 95, 97
Alibis, deceptive, 3, 66–67
American Academy of Matrimonial
  Lawyers, 23(n22)
American Bar Association, 22(n1), 78,
  93, 109
Applied morality or ethics, 29
Attorney-client privilege, 52
Autonomy of client, as moral
  justification for lawyer behavior,
  38–40, 43
Avoidance of knowledge,
  53–54

"Beauty contests" for lawyers, 90
Bell, Griffin, 79
Beneficence, duty of, 28, 31
Billable hours, 101
Billing by lawyers, 101
Blackmail, 9, 71
Blood tests, 2
Bok, Sissela, 29
Brandeis, Louis, 87
Burden of proof, 18, 65
Business, practice of law as, 99

Canons of Professional Ethics (1908),
  22(n1), 93
Child abuse, 15, 61
Civil liability, defined, 7
Civil wrong, lawyer counseling and
  assisting, 7, 19, 45
Civility among lawyers, decline of, 103
Clergy, privilege, 52
Competition among lawyers, 86, 90, 92
Confidentiality, lawyers duty of
  client crimes, 14
  client fraud, 14
  criminal defense, 17, 46, 65
  defined, 56
  exceptions, 20, 56, 57
  injustice caused by, 13, 20, 58, 63
  justification for, 56, 59
  personal commitment to client, 59
  professional commitment, 59
  prosecutor, 65
  relationship to perjury, 58, 59, 62
Contingent fees, 102–103
Contract law, duty of parties to disclose
  information, 13, 64
Contracts
  breach of, 7, 44–46
  counseling breach, 7, 19, 44–46
  inserting illegal clause, 10, 72
Corporations, lawyers for, 89–92
Costs, legal, 90
Cox, Archibald, 88
Cramton, Roger, 88
Criminal conduct
  lawyer counseling and assisting, 7,
    19, 45–46
  lawyer describing consequences of, 6,
    69
Criminal defense, 42–43, 65, 67

Criminal law, defined, 7
Cross-examination
    discrediting truthful witness, 2, 66
    hardball tactics, 104
Custody disputes, 9, 71

Depositions, 77
Dilatory tactics, 5, 69
Disclosure, duty of, 11, 13, 64, 73, 78
Discovery, 76
    abuses, 77, 104
Discrimination, 28, 31
Dishonesty, 9
Distributive justice, 31
Drugs, 34

Economic analysis of law, 49(n41)
Economic self-interest of lawyers, 101
Efficient breach of contract, 49(n41)
Elite law firms, 89
Environmental regulations, 6, 69
Ethics, applied, 29
Evidence
    destruction of, 21
    unreasonable search, 52
Expert witnesses, shopping for, 54
Exploitation of clients, 101–103
    contingent fees, 102
Explosion of law, 90

Federal Rules of Civil Procedure,
    23(n8, 15), 76, 78
Fees, contingent, 102
Fidelity, moral duty of, 28, 30
Fiduciary, lawyer as, 18, 92, 101, 103
Fifth Amendment privilege against self-
    incrimination, 52
First Amendment freedom of
    expression, 17, 36, 93
Fourth Amendment protection against
    unreasonable searches, 52
Frankel, Marvin, 23, 53, 80
Fraud, definition of, 7
Fraudulent conduct
    counseling and assisting, 7, 10, 59,
        71, 72
    describing consequences of, 6
Free market, legal services, 39, 41, 98

Freedman, Monroe, 22(n2), 54
Frivolous legal action, 5, 69

General counsel, 89–90
Goldman, Alan, 42
Good Samaritan, no duty to be, 63

Harassment, 2
Hardball practices, 103
Harm, active and passive, 62
Hired gun, 85, 89, 91
Hoffman, David, 87
Holmes, Oliver Wendell, 49(n40)
Homicide, unprosecuted, 15, 60
House counsel for corporations, 89–91

Illegal clause, 10, 72
Illegality, defined, 45
Immoral law, 34
Inconsistent positions by lawyer, 12,
    74
Independent lawyer, 86–89, 91, 98
Insanity, 67
Intentions, misrepresenting, 9, 71
Interrogatories, 77
Intuitionism, 28
Investigators, 9, 72

Judge, role morality of, 34
Jury, nullification by, 35, 48
Justice, duty of, 28, 31
Justice theory of representation, 75

Kant, Immanuel, 28
Keeton, Robert E., 24(n24)
Knowing, defined, 3, 116

Landlords, 10, 72
Law firms, large corporate
    current competition among, 90
    history, 89
    insecurity and fluidity, 91
Layman, lawyer's dealing with, 11, 20,
    73
Legal ethics, 1, 5
Legal system, as moral justification for
    lawyer behavior, 36

Legislature, legal objectives determined by, 36, 51
Leveraging of associates by law firms, 101
Liberalism, classical, 31, 41
Lies, 8, 19, 29, 31, 70
Lincoln, Abraham, 87, 92
Lord Broughham, 18
Luban, David, 43–44

Mailings, targeted, 95–97
Marketing of legal services, 90, 97, 100
Means
  justification for immoral, 51
  lawyer determines, 21
Media, use of by trial lawyers, 104
Misrepresentation, 8, 70
Money-consciousness of lawyers, 100
Moral conflicts, 30
Moral conversation with client, 40
Morality
  applied, 29
  principles of, 28
  role of lawyer, 35

Natural law, 29
Nazis, 17, 36
Negligence, 10, 19, 45, 73
Negotiations, 8, 9, 70, 71
  settlement authority, 8
Nondisclosure as fraud, 64
Nonmaleficence, duty of, 28, 30
Nullification by jury, 35, 48

Objectives, client determines, 21
O'Connor, Sandra Day, 96, 97, 99

Pepper, Stephen, 38–40, 43, 44
Perjury
  duty not to present, 2, 3, 19, 66, 67
  duty to correct, 20, 57
Physician-patient privilege, 52
Probe, no duty to, 3, 20, 58, 68

Professional responsibility, 1
Professionalism
  advertising, 94
  decline of, 86
  defined, 92
Promises
  contract as, 45
  moral duty to keep, 28, 30, 33
Proof, standards in trials, 67
Prosecutor, discretion of, 35

Rawls, John, 28, 31
Rehnquist, William, 96
Religious morality, 29
Representation
  accepting or declining, 51, 86
  termination, 6, 86
Role morality
  of judge, 34
  of lawyer, 35
  of military, 38
  of parents, 37
Rule 11 of Federal Rules of Civil Procedure, 23(n8,15)
Rule 26 of Federal Rules of Civil Procedure, 78
Rules governing lawyers determined by courts, 32

Scalia, Antonin, 79, 96
Searches, constitutional protection against unreasonable, 52
Self-incrimination, privilege against, 2, 52
Settlement authority, 8
Sharswood, George, 86
Situation ethics, 29
Small firm practice, 92
Social contract, 29
Solicitation of clients by lawyers
  by mail, 95, 97
  in-person, 96
Souter, David, 79
Sporting theory of representation, 75, 105

Spousal privilege, 52
Statutes of limitations, 15, 36, 87
Stewart, Potter, 99
Subterfuge, 9, 72

Tactics, lawyer determines, 21
Tenants, 10, 72
Thomas, Clarence, 79
Torts, 45
Truth
  avoidance of, 53
  in nonlegal disciplines, 53–55
  litigation as means of determining,
    52–55

Utilitarianism, 28

Warnock, Geoffrey, 27
Wasserstrom, Richard, 37, 40, 42, 55
Welfare state, 31
Wills, 4
Wilson, Woodrow, 88
Witnesses
  expert, 54
  impeaching credibility, 2, 19, 66
  improper questions, 104
  preparation of, 4, 19, 68
  presenting questionable testimony, 3,
    19, 68
  truthful but misleading, 3, 66
Wolfram, Charles, 22(n2)

Zeal, lawyer's duty of, 18